EVENT MANAGEMENT IN LEISURE AND TOURISM

EVENT MANAGEMENT IN LEISURE AND TOURISM

DAVID C. WATT

ADDISON WESLEY LONGMAN

Pearson Education Limited
Edinburgh Gate
Harlow, Essex CM20 2JE, England
and Associated Companies throughout the world.

Published in the United States of America
by Addison Wesley Longman Publishing, New York

First published 1998
Second impression 2000
Third impression 2001

ISBN 0 582 35706-3

Visit Pearson Education on the world wide web at
http://www.pearsoneduc.com

British Library Cataloguing-in-Publication Data

A catalogue record for this book is
available from the British Library.

Set by 35 in 9.5/12 pt Garamond Light
Printed in Malaysia, PP

Contents

CHAPTER EIGHT *Sources of Help, Advice and Support*

About the Author

David C. Watt is director of the Leisure Training Consortium, a consultancy working on a wide range of leisure projects but specialising in staff training. Formerly a leisure manager and sports administrator, as well as a writer and lecturer, David has worked in the private, public and voluntary sectors, including six years as president of a voluntary organisation. He has managed and organised many events, including caravan rallies, tourist visits, careers exhibitions, trade displays, a radio convention, seminars and meetings as well as literally hundreds of sporting events from local to international level. This is his third book giving advice and knowledge to event management practitioners and students. He has run well over a hundred training courses on the subject of events for a range of paid and voluntary staff, as well as lecturing at various further and higher education establishments.

Preface

This book is written by someone who is in the event management business for others in the same field. Someone who knows the commitment, effort and nerve required to get events successfully completed. There is a distinct lack of useful texts on event management, and this one attempts to play a major part in remedying the situation. It aims to provide a practical guide to event management, after having considered some of the relevant background concepts.

The intention is to keep the book succinct, while still being generically appropriate to the leisure and tourism field. It would have been possible to insert considerably more information, but what is contained should be a helpful guide for people operating in the field of event organisation. The text, the advice, the methodology and the examples should also be of use to the student of events and their management.

The leisure and tourism field is immense and diverse, ranging from arts to zoos, from antique shows to quizzes, and from acrobatics to sponsored walks. This leads to major difficulties in applying organisational principles to all areas; and so it must remain, but anyone setting out to achieve a successful event should find this book very helpful.

It is written for practitioners by a practitioner, someone who has organised hundreds of events and still organises around fifty events at various levels every year. It is hoped that people coming to this book with only minimal organisational experience, or perhaps none, will be able to put together successful events at a range of levels, from local to international.

Naturally, the principles outlined are of considerable importance to students of the business, and the specific case studies and practical implementation documents will set them off in the right direction. The self-assessment questions may also prove particularly useful.

The leisure field is very broad, but the principles and practical examples apply to a variety of situations. Although several of the examples are drawn from sport, it is not to suggest that the underlying principles of event organisation are limited uniquely to sport and physical activities. Indeed, the similarities far outweigh any specific differences that may exist between sports, arts, seminars, festivals, conferences, etc. There is no doubt that conference organisers and arts display organisers could benefit from the experience of the organisers of major sporting occasions and vice versa. There may be a real difference in the specific technicalities, but the fundamental principles are universal.

Additionally, it is intended that the lessons and principles highlighted in this text will be equally relevant to organisers from the public, private and voluntary sectors. The similarities in provision methods far outweigh the differences in priority, emphasis and *raison d'être* which may exist.

There are occasions when operators from any sector could benefit from working together and learning from each other's experience and expertise. Sharing knowledge of each other's priorities and practice in the setting up of events, exhibitions, seminars and conferences will be extremely beneficial to both parties. The advantages of a shared experience will surface regularly. Learn from anyone; project managers in all spheres can always share 'traumatic' experiences to increase mutual knowledge.

It may be that the search for a general approach to principles and practices which are applicable to operators in such a wide-ranging field has left some specific areas a little bare. It is inevitable within a text which aims to cover a number of general areas that one or two specific details for specialist organisers may need to be more fully covered elsewhere. There will always be specific technical details for an event which must be specially considered, and planned for, in consultation with technical experts.

The specific technical knowledge required to stage a Rembrandt exhibition will only come from specific art experts, but the establishment of the event can be done by a generalist event organiser. In real terms, technical knowledge is often only a small part of staging a major event. Hopefully, with assistance from this publication, individuals and groups will feel better prepared for the task they face. If they provide the enthusiasm and the commitment, then this text should provide the necessary advice to achieve a worthwhile conclusion.

Throughout the book, the emphasis is on actually equipping the organiser with practical advice to plan, prepare and implement an event successfully; and to guide students in their studies. Bear in mind that the word *event* is used in its widest sense, because the advice given applies equally to theatrical, sporting, artistic or tourist occasions. Remember that many more have trodden the path before you and survived. With hard work, good organisation and a sense of humour, so can you!

Good luck!

David C. Watt
March 1998

Acknowledgements

The help of many has been essential to pulling together this book on what is a very diverse area. The author is grateful to them all, in particular:

- Earle Bloomfield, Kidsplay UK Ltd, Exeter
- British Tourist Authority
- Nigel Buckler, West Country Tourist Board, Exeter
- Richard Callicot, Birmingham City Council
- Giselle Coffey, Sales and Marketing Manager, Victoria Conference Centre, British Columbia
- Countryside Commission
- Paul Emery, Research Coordinator, Division of Sport and Recreation, University of Northumbria at Newcastle
- Gordon District Council
- Nigel Gough, Nova International, Newcastle upon Tyne
- Gar Holohan, Holohan Architects
- Iain Jackson, East Kilbride District Council (now South Lanarkshire)
- Martin Morton, Sheffield City Council
- George Imber, GM Imber Insurance Brokers Limited
- ILAM Information Centre
- International Association of Amusement Parks and Attractions
- Robin Ireland, Director, Healthstart Limited
- David Leslie, Reader, Glasgow Caledonian University
- Keith Leslie, Senior Recreation Officer, Aberdeenshire Council
- Mike Nutley, Editor, Leisure Week
- Graham Ross, English Sports Council (formerly of the Scottish Athletics Federation)
- Nigel Rowe MBE, Manager, DML Sports and Social Club
- Scottish Gymnastics Association
- Sue Stayte, Marketing Director, ILAM

- Brian Stocks, National Indoor Arena, Birmingham
- Anne Sudder, Events and Recreation Officer, The Highland Council
- United States Gymnastics Federation
- Steve Warner, Sales Director, Insurex Expo-sure Limited
- David Wilkinson, Wilkinson Group, Ontario, Canada
- Fiona Williams, Hertfordshire Council
- Mike Wilson, formerly of Gameplan, Edinburgh
- Alastair Wylie, Wylie and Reid PR, Glasgow
- Kelly for her patience and her word processing and Maggie for her constant support
- Everyone who gave me the time to get it all together

Some of those listed above gave permission for me to use their material in an earlier publication, *Leisure and Tourism Events Management and Organisation Manual*. Every effort has been made to trace the owners of the copyright material in order to reclear permission for this book, however, in a few cases this has proved impossible and I take this opportunity to offer my apologies to any copyright holders whose rights I may have unwittingly infringed.

Chapter One

Introduction to Events

The dictionary defines an *event* as 'anything that happens, as distinguished from anything that exists' or 'an occurrence, especially one of great importance'. These definitions specify the subject of this text – events – things of significance that happen. They are very wide definitions, but they have to be all-embracing to allow for their innate universality in leisure and tourism, something considered a little later. They can range from local village events to international spectacles featuring participants from throughout the world.

Further definitions:

A special event is a one-off happening designed to meet specific needs at any given time.

Local community events may be defined as an activity established to involve the local population in a shared experience to their mutual benefits.

(*Wilkinson*)

Or take Goldblatt's definition:

A special event recognises an unique moment in time with ceremony and ritual to satisfy specific needs.

The definition can be flexible to suit different situations, but exactly what is meant in terms of a special events department, or an events officer, or an organising group must be clearly established before starting on specific events and the work they require.

A variety of events

In leisure, tourism and related fields, events are extremely diverse:

- artistic performances
- carnivals
- festivals
- training days
- trade exhibitions
- fetes
- sporting competitions, tournaments and displays
- art displays
- firework displays
- environmental days
- war games

- civic galas
- celebrity appearances
- agricultural shows
- open days
- garden displays
- band contests
- open days
- caravan rallies
- boat trips
- historic tours
- museum displays
- careers exhibitions
- music festivals
- marathons
- educational seminars
- air displays
- Highland games
- sponsored walks
- dog shows
- round-the-world races
- pageants
- theatrical performances
- nature tours
- motoring rallies
- royal tournaments
- street parties
- garden parties
- car boot sales
- parades
- town shows

A long list, and still it has many omissions – the area is so large it would be impossible to detail all the possibilities. In any case, someone is constantly devising new projects and organisers all over the place are adding to the list.

It is important to recognise this diversity and treat every event as different; each event has its own characteristics and requirements to be identified and met. Regarding each venture as exactly the same is dangerous and can lead to poor organisation, through failure to consider all the relevant factors.

It happens

An event is something that 'happens' not just 'exists', and here is the biggest issue – somebody has to make it happen. Successful events only come about through action – some individual or group of individuals getting things done. This applies to all events (little or large) and applies to every last detail within each event; attention to detail is vital (as will be seen later).

Every single thing that needs to happen has to be made to happen by someone initiating the action. One of the key steps is to identify all the tasks which have to be accomplished, and all of them have to be carried out for a successful event to occur.

The importance of events

It is very important for event organisers (who may become blasé as they set up their twenty-third art exhibition) to remember that for many involved it may be their first. For the patrons, every event is of major significance or they wouldn't be there. For the spectator it may be the thrill of a lifetime, for the participant their biggest opportunity to date, even though the organiser may see it as the last event in a long series.

Properly done, events can be a great thrill; but poorly done, they can be an unpleasant experience for all concerned. Every effort has got to go into ensuring everything is right every time. Perhaps it's easy to raise commitment for an international seminar, but the next day's business meeting may be just as vital to its participants – their jobs might be on the line! And so might the organisers', if it's not right!

Difficult though it may be, each event has got to get all the attention it requires. All events and all their customers are important and they deserve the best treatment possible. Yet each event is unique, and one of the key considerations is to identify the differences and how to handle them successfully. Although this book highlights common aspects and suggests general approaches to organising events, it does not attempt to treat them all the same. The organiser has got to identify the exact nature of their task, so they can analyse correctly the detailed work to be done.

There will be similarities in every village fete to be organised, but it could vary in some way depending on factors like these:

- geographic location
- size of population
- age of population
- number of voluntary organisations
- affluence of the community
- ability of organisers
- nature of the site
- facilities and equipment available

A fete may seem like a fairly straightforward event, but the larger it becomes and the more peculiarities it acquires, the more complex it will be to organise. It is vital to recognise the unique features when organising an event.

Similarities between events

Events certainly have unique features but they also have similarities. The basic principles and general practicalities of event organisation can be applied to all events. Some organisers try to reinvent the wheel; they fail to learn organisational lessons from others doing a similar job. This may derive from a certain personal and 'professional' pride, as well as a feeling that certain areas in leisure and tourism are quite different. The fact is there are more generic similarities than individual differences.

Art organisers can learn from sports organisers and vice versa. Their technical and specialist requirements may be different, but they will have many universal needs. Among other common issues, both will need to consider funding, facilities, transport, marketing and staffing. They will face common problems and they can apply common solutions.

Detailed event characteristics are important and must be examined, but likenesses between events are more common and they need to be examined as well. The concepts and practical examples of this book will prove that sound ideas and logical action will benefit operators in all project areas.

The complexity of an event

The importance of an event should not be judged simply by its level, local or international; its standard, novice or advanced; or simply the numbers taking part. But these issues will affect the event in many ways.

Funding will be needed for all events, but the amount will vary drastically depending on the nature of the occasion. Media attention and media provision will vary enormously, as will sponsorship openings and many other considerations.

The perceived level of complexity should not affect the need to think an event through; but inevitably it will affect the amount of time, personnel and commitment required. When bidding for a major event, it is essential to be doubly certain that all the funding and other resources are guaranteed; more of this later. Remember what happened to the 1986 Commonwealth games! It is very easy to come to the brink of disaster if you underestimate the onerous demands of a major event. All too frequently some bright spark will decide 'we must have an event' without considering the consequences or the amount of work involved.

Key steps to a successful event

Although events vary, most of them follow the same vital stages of organisation. These stages are progressive, and only in exceptional circumstances should any of them be omitted:

Step 1 Ask the initial event questions.

Step 2 Clarify and establish the event aims and objectives.

Step 3 Carry out a feasibility study and evaluate the results; produce a written report and outline brief where necessary.

Step 4 Establish planning and implementation methodologies and draw up a time schedule.

Step 5 Secure finance and any required approvals.

Step 6 Launch the event into the public area.

Step 7 Establish operating structures and recruit key personnel.

Step 8 Carry out all necessary preplanning and establish appropriate control systems.

Step 9 Achieve pre-event preparation through a trained efficient workforce and a good communication system.

Step 10 Publicise the event.

Step 11 Complete a comprehensive last-minute double-check on all arrangements.

Step 12 Carry out the event as per plan and contingency strategy.

Step 13 Review and evaluate the event after completion and finalise accounts.

Step 14 Prepare a detailed report for appropriate personnel and future use.

Organising an event is like baking a cake. It will be rich and enjoyable if the ingredients are well closen.

Ask the right questions

Before starting to organise any event, it is vital to answer the following questions regarding the concept. If you can't answer them all, it may be best not to start:

- *Why* do we need to or want to hold an event?
- *What* is the precise nature of the event?
- *When* will it be held?
- *Where* will it be held?
- *How* can it be achieved?
- *What cost* is involved?
- *Who* will organise?
    will attend?
    will watch?
    will participate?
    will pay?

- How will the event be *publicised*?
- Will it interest the *media*?
- Is it attractive to a *sponsor*?
- Are there any *political* implications?
- Is there another *similar* event?
- What happens *afterwards*?
- What's the *next* step?

Other questions may need to be answered in specific situations, or with larger or more complex events, but the whole of this list must be considered before embarking on any project.

Why?

Why? is probably the most important question of all. There has to be a very real reason for the event if you are to spend time, energy and finance on it. The commitment required to achieve events successfully is considerable and it can only be gained through a clear unity of purpose for everyone involved.

Many people have an idea which initially seems sensible but they don't have the real motivation or drive that comes from a specific purpose for staging it. There has got to be a genuine target and meaning for all the efforts of the individuals involved. Major events and events that employ large numbers of staff have the greatest need for an aim that encourages team spirit and unity of purpose.

When Sheffield hosted the World Student Games in 1991, it had several aims:

- To play an integral part in the economic regeneration of the area.
- To heighten Sheffield's profile, nationally and internationally.
- To identify Sheffield's potential as a major sporting venue.
- To encourage local participation in sport and collaboration in the games.
- To promote relocation to Sheffield for seminars, conferences, etc.
- To leave the city a legacy of world-class facilities, as it heads into the next century.

And Manchester has its own aims for the 2002 Commonwealth games. A September 1997 update from Manchester 2002 includes the following projections:

- Significant long-lasting benefits from capital investment in new facilities, principally the new stadium in Eastlands.
- More than 4000 permanent new jobs will be created as a result of hosting the games in 2002. The stadium and associated developments alone could generate up to 2800 permanent new jobs.
- Significant employment will be generated from organising the games. Over the seven-year build-up, employment generated in Manchester and the North West region would be approximately 500 person-years. This excludes the use of volunteers.
- Further benefits will accrue from other areas of the operating budget, such as installing and operating communications equipment, running the games village, marketing, etc. Expenditure on these areas will generate economic benefits for many local companies.

- Significant benefits to Manchester and the North West will arise from additional visitor expenditure. The increase in tourism expenditure for the 1994 Commonwealth games in Victoria was at least £25 million. If a similar level was achieved, this could support more than 6000 person-years of employment in new or existing jobs in the region.
- More than £100 million is expected to flow into the region from a combination of the above elements during the seven-year build-up.

It goes on to cite other benefits:

- After-use of new facilities.
- Enhanced visitor numbers and spending resulting from increased awareness of Manchester and the region.
- Potential to attract new inward investment as a result of Manchester's enhanced image.
- Nationally the games will have an economic impact from raised awareness across the world.

All individuals involved must also know the aims for the event and the aims for themselves; the demands on them will be high, so they must be dedicated to the overall purpose.

What?

It is essential to be quite explicit about what has to be organised. Any lack of detail in defining the nature of the event will cause problems later, in identifying exactly what has to be done, and where it can or should be held. For major events this may well have to be expanded into a bid document specifying exactly what will be achieved, how and where.

Even smaller-scale ventures need a clear picture of what is intended. Only with a clear picture will sponsors, participants, etc., support the proposal. This may seem a straightforward idea, but getting a product wrong will weaken its marketing potential, and vagueness in an event's definition will later produce uncertainty in all its aspects.

When?

Firstly, make sure the event is scheduled far enough away for you to achieve it. Consider the month of the year, the day of the week, the hour of the day, and the relationship to other similar events in local, national or international calendars. A clash can be disastrous for all involved.

Timing is particularly important if television or other major media coverage is being pursued. It is a good idea to speak to the media before setting an exact date for major events; they can help to avoid clashes and give an early indication of the possibilities. A sports event that clashes with World Cup soccer, an arts event that competes with the Edinburgh Festival, both are nightmares for obtaining media coverage. If possible, have some alternative dates and make enquiries to see which looks best.

The date should also fit logically into the activity's annual calendar and be at a time which will maximise benefits to the participants and the organisational culture.

Where?

Geographical location is important and so is a venue; they can be vital to success. An event must have convenient transport links, both public and private, and its venue should be easy to find. Wandering about lost and late is nobody's idea of fun. An event run in a cold, uncomfortable venue is unlikely to be a great success. And otherwise successful events will only be attended once if the venue is poor. Customers in this sophisticated age expect a high standard of venue specification and comfort.

Some venues in the United Kingdom have limited facilities, such as dressing-rooms; they cannot support full high-level provision. Give careful thought to everything desired for the event, then choose the venue accordingly.

How?

We can have an ideal venue and a great concept, but if we haven't got a workable method, then the first two items mean nothing. We need the appropriate resources to stage the event, otherwise it will be impossible. We must have the personnel, structure, support services and overall commitment if the event is to proceed successfully.

The mechanics are vital; if they don't exist, there is no point in proceeding. The logistics must also be within the scope of the central group or individual; being ambitious is fine, but unrealistic is dangerous.

What cost?

To be successful an event needs funding. It is immensely dangerous, and perhaps financially damaging, to go ahead with an event without knowing how it will be funded. A detailed budget of anticipated income and expenditure must be prepared before starting any project; it must try to cover every possible area but still leave enough room to cope with any emergency.

Who?

Perhaps this is *the* key issue. Every event needs personnel. At a major manifestation, there may be quite a complex organisational structure of committees involving many personnel; whereas local events may be staged by only a few people, sometimes even just one person.

Effective leadership, organisation and hard work is paramount, whatever the number of organisers. An event organiser is a key figure who combines the following roles:

- administrator
- planner
- information coordinator
- presentation specialist
- management consultant
- personality
- humorist
- powerhouse
- field operative
- decision maker
- crisis manager
- people person
- saint

And there are other people that need to be considered, such as audience members and fundraisers:

- watchers
- attenders
- participants
- sponsors
- political supporters

Without an audience or clients for the promotion, the efforts of the organisers are wasted. If there isn't a clearly identified target audience then there should be no event. Old or young, dog lovers or pigeon fanciers, music or theatre supporters, the target must be quite clear and the event must be planned for them.

Another question is, who is going to finance the event costs? This *must* be clearly identified, not believed or hoped for, but known before progressing any detailed work.

Other questions

Other issues which have to examined include just about all those listed in the checklists at the back of this book. However, items such as media interest, publicity methods and the possibility of sponsorship will require a long think at an early stage.

Feasibility study

A feasibility study is an examination of all the appropriate items required for an event. Every event requires lots of questions to be asked and answered, but it need not take long. A small event may be covered by an informal chat with a colleague. The crucial point is that feasibility must have some genuine consideration.

Planning comes next

> *Failure to plan is planning to fail.*
>
> *(Anon)*

Having asked all the relevant questions (and maybe others) in a fairly general way, and having come up with positive answers, the next step is more detailed event planning.

Planning is 'determining what has to be done and how'. The amount of planning that goes into an event can vary considerably with the complexity and perceived importance of the occasion, but some planning will always be required.

The golden rule is that every event must be planned; if an event is to happen, it can only do so as the result of carefully planned action. The steps for success have to be identified and carried out in a prearranged fashion.

> *The best preparation for good work tomorrow is to do good work today.*
>
> *(Elbert Hubbard)*

Planning is the process which identifies aims and objectives, and establishes the methods of achieving them. Project planning should be undertaken in a structured and logical manner (Fig. 1.1). There are lots of excellent examples of methodology from other industries like construction or information technology. Leisure event organisers should learn from them.

    Remember   **P**roper
                Planning
                Promotes
                Perfect
                Performance

Figure 1.1   The event-planning process

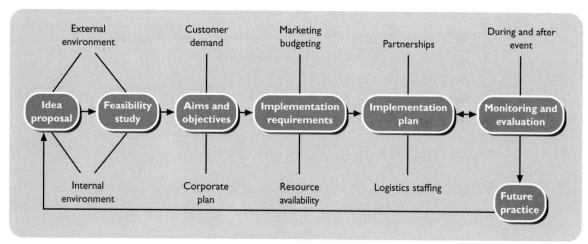

A starting point

Some questions that should be asked before embarking on any event were suggested earlier, but this was an informal assessment. A much more detailed investigation should be carried out for any large or costly event.

Step 1   The aims and objectives of staging the particular event must be clearly identified and stated.

Step 2   A feasibility study should be undertaken, asking questions (like those earlier) in a much more factual way. It should examine the exact methods of achieving the event and it should definitely identify any possible sources of funding.

Depending on the level of the event, these two steps can be performed in a variety of ways, ranging from consideration by a small informal group to the engagement of specialist consultants. Investigations into an event often have to be carried out over a short timescale. If the event is found to be justifiable and worthwhile, the investigation should go on to suggest how it can be achieved.

The feasibility study, with its positive outcome, should outline how to achieve the event; it should detail structures, personnel requirements, financial sources and an event achievement timetable. This will allow the more detailed event planning and implementation to proceed, as long as enough time is allowed. It is always dangerous to embark on any event if the timescale is inadequate. Problems often occur quite naturally, it is inadvisable to introduce time pressure from the very start.

Part of a plan

For events to be the most effective they are best set within the context of an organisational plan. Regardless of the size or nature of the organisation and its activity, events should be provided as part of the ethos and function of the whole business, not just a random fulfilment of an idea.

Events take individual and organisational time and commitment to deliver properly, so they have to be justified as a real part of an overall plan. They must fit in with organisational aims and objectives; they must be coordinated across all parts of the organisation; and they must be worthwhile in future.

There must be a beneficial follow-on and part of a strategic plan; indeed, there should be an events strategy specifying the following items from the agency's viewpoint:

- The purpose of having events.
- What aims and objectives they should have.
- What staff will be involved.
- How they will be coordinated.
- Who will take the lead role.

The aims of an event

Through being an integral part of an overall strategy, events should have a key role in achieving organisational aims, such as increasing the awareness of an issue among the general public in north-west England.

The overall events policy should also clearly state the general aims for all events the organisation stages, e.g.

- To provide for the local population's entertainment.
- To raise funds for the company.

A strong indication of viewpoint and policy can come through such an aim. For example, if the key focus is to promote customer care, then an appropriate aim might be this one, people get more from every event than they expected.

Almost from the outset it is essential to establish a very clear aim, or set of aims, for every single event. There are hundreds of possible examples:

- To attract more visitors to the town.
- To encourage local participation in sport.
- To promote the visual arts.
- To put Wormsley-on-Sea on the world map.

The list is almost endless. There may be one aim or several aims; but however many, it is essential to have them clearly specified during the search for finance and staff.

A clear vision is crucial if we want people to sign up, people from sponsors to car park attendants. If there are no aims, what is the point in proceeding? Sheffield's detailed aims for the Universiade (pp. 13–21) show how the city has a clear idea of the event and its purpose.

The objectives of an event

If you don't know where you are going you will probably end up somewhere else.
(Dr Laurence J Peter and Raymond Hill)

Having established the *raison d'être* for the whole event, it will be necessary to break it into more manageable steps of measurable achievement – objectives.

It is vital that objectives are set, agreed and understood by everyone involved. Everyone must commit themselves to accomplishing these targets; this will lead to clear focus, coordinated effort and unity of purpose. Objectives should be SMART:

Specific to the event.

Measurable in statistical terms.

Agreed (or achievable) by those involved.

Realistic (or relevant) to the resources available.

Timed around the event schedule.

And objectives should be simple and unambiguous; they should avoid causing confusion and misunderstanding or communicating incorrect messages.

Events can certainly be 'managed by objectives', as long as they are clear and achievable. It is most effective to set these markers and then work towards reaching each one. An event is an accumulation of these stages and is best achieved when each is accomplished in a logical, progressive way. Critical path analysis (illustrated later) is the ultimate expression of this method.

The precise definition of objectives also assists greatly in establishing an organisational structure. It allows each individual or committee to be given a number of their own specific targets (sub-objectives) which they are responsible for attaining. This will further reflect the need for everyone to work together, as many objectives will inevitably be interdependent.

It is important that the objectives are appropriate, simple, clear, unambiguous and achievable. In the financial area there must be precise estimates and budgeting for each, dates and deadlines must be set, and the critical steps to fulfilment must be identified.

Characteristics of the best events

Before examining the factors involved in achieving our overall aim or goal, let us consider what makes for a good event. The most important elements are:

1. A clear vision and a definite purpose for everyone's efforts.

2. Clear SMART objectives to which everyone is committed.

3. An appropriate, flexible organisational structure able to achieve specific tasks, but retaining an overall unity of purpose.

4. Committed personnel, willing to 'go the step beyond'.

5. A leader of calibre, authority and personality.

6. Precise detailed planning carried out and documented within an appropriate timescale.

7. A coordinated team effort operating within budget limits, drawing on all available resources.

8. Efficient lines of communication.

9. A good public image.

10. Effective publicity and presentation, and built-in contingency plans.

11. A total commitment to customer care.

12. Efficient ongoing control and monitoring systems.

13. An atmosphere of unity, focus, hard work, humour and enthusiasm.

14. Good post-event evaluation.

Centrality of events

Smaller events and the events programme can be very important to major manifestations like a garden festival, but their importance is often underestimated by main event organisers. The Glasgow Garden Festival ended up being programmed and piloted by the events team and the centre of the whole manifestation was in fact the events programme. The main attraction was the events programme, and the impetus to the festival was the events programme.

The garden festival was not a major flower show or an environmental exhibition, as many people saw it, but rather a series of events located within the environment and the surrounds of the garden displays. Few people would have come had it been only a massive flower show, but many came to see the events performed by sports, arts and entertainment groups. The pipe band performances and the acrobatics displays were as central to the success of the garden festival as the plants.

Besides being a crucial part of the whole programme, the events were a key element which considerably helped the overall planning. The diary, the booking sheets, the programmes, the staffing arrangements, the security and other systems that built up because of the festival events, became the basic operational working scheme for the festival itself.

Events and promotions form a key part of such major spectacles as garden festivals. They should not be seen as an extra, but as something which is absolutely crucial and central to the whole project, assisting in the planning and successful implementation of the whole festival. Events are important, not just in themselves, but in the implications they hold for everyone else involved.

The centrality and significance of events to other concepts like urban regeneration has been recognised even by the UK government, although it has been very slow to react. John Major committed the last Conservative government to spending £55 million to assist Manchester in staging its bid for the Olympic games in the year 2000 by constructing a velodrome and assisting its organising group. In making this announcement, he said that it was 'not only a recognition of the importance of the Olympic Games, but the building of the new facilities required would play a key role in the economic regeneration of the Eastern Manchester area'. The bid may have failed but the vision remains, and now the Commonwealth games will provide a lesser, but similar opportunity in 2002.

A similar view was taken by Michael Heseltine when, after the Toxteth riots in Liverpool, his solution was to bring a garden festival to Liverpool two years after the troubles, in order to give the city back some heart and some faith in itself. The garden festival concept lasted for another decade visiting Stoke-on-Trent, Glasgow, Gateshead and Ebbw Vale, in addition to Liverpool. On each occasion this major event/promotion has helped with the image and self-confidence of the host town or city.

Being the venue for a major international event has been a cause for celebration in many, many places and has helped put places on the world map, e.g. Glasgow and its cultural links or Indianapolis and its 500-mile race.

What do you need for success?

This question is often asked, but sadly there is no easy or magic answer. Certainly all the items listed in this book will be needed, but also a considerable slice of luck, good judgement, etc. However, here are some of the things that may be important:

- appropriate implementation mechanisms
- attention to detail
- budgeting
- business plan
- charismatic personality
- clear structure
- commitment to serving the participants and customers
- contingency plan
- creativity and innovation
- customer care
- detailed programming
- efficient time management
- emergency procedures
- entertainment
- evaluation and control
- excellent communications
- good decision making
- good interpersonal relationships
- good management
- good motivation
- hard work and enthusiasm
- large number of volunteers
- large slice of luck
- leadership
- logistical planning
- market research
- measurable targets
- media interest
- planning and documentation
- political support
- positive image
- quality provision
- resources and facilities
- responsiveness to change
- sense of humour
- SMART objectives
- strong leadership
- strong vision
- teamwork
- top-quality committed people

The Sheffield process

Introduction and background to events in Sheffield

Beyond the World Snooker Championships and occasional professional football matches, until 1990 the city had little involvement with national or international sports events. As such the city did not have the opportunity to develop gradually in the events market in the way that Birmingham, Edinburgh, Gateshead and London had. However, the 1991 World Student Games (WSG), the biggest multisport event to be ever held in this country, has changed this.

The new facility developments and the WSG, required a pre-games events programme in order to trial the facilities and prepare organisations for the games. In the mid 1980s there were extensive job losses in the traditional steel and heavy engineering industries, mainly due to the introduction of new technology and automation. In turn this left a number of former works sites derelict and in need of strategic investment. In the late 1980s, part of the overall vision for Sheffield 2000 included state-of-the-art leisure development, and international sporting events were seen as part of this, being identified as a means of profiling and promoting the city. It was anticipated that they would also contribute towards and stimulate the local economy. In fact, seven years later the city is committed to profiling and promoting itself by means of an events-led strategy.

By the early 1990s, Sheffield had invested £139 million in high-quality state-of-the-art sports facilities in order to successfully stage the WSG and so the impetus generated by this event would enable the city to stage other major national and international events. In turn the city was also able to develop skills and expertise for event organisation, so it could make full use of the facilities that remained after the games, all of which are very important.

As a result of this, in 1990 the city council appointed an officer within its existing Sports Development Unit with specific responsibility for the development and coordination of a major sports events programme as a build-up to the WSG and then beyond. To emphasise the city council's long-term commitment to the staging of major sporting events, the team has now increased to five full-time officers. This small team, now recognised as the Sheffield Events Unit, works within the Leisure Services Directorate of Sheffield City Council. They are responsible for event acquisition and procurement in addition to the effective operational delivery of the event. The unit acts as a first port of call for governing bodies of sport and event promoters who wish to stage their prestigious event in Sheffield.

Each individual event is evaluated against the criteria set by the city for staging events. In order to evaluate the success and benefits to the city through its major sports events programme, clearly defined aims and objectives have been established and the criteria set. The city's strategy for the attraction and staging of sports events is straightforward. Key aims and objectives have been set and each event enquiry is matched against predetermined criteria. This indicates the suitability of the event to the city in terms of its potential in achieving and satisfying those key aims and objectives.

Although the Sheffield Events Unit is an integral part of Sheffield City Council it enjoys excellent working relationships with its business partners in the city, including Destination Sheffield, Sheffield's chosen vehicle for city marketing and promotion, and other private sector companies. Over the past seven years, the unit has gained unrivalled experience in the staging of sports events. Four of its current team were involved in the World Student Games, the European Swimming Championships and the Special Olympics, three of the biggest sports events ever staged in the United Kingdom. The unit also played a key role in the management of Euro '96, assisting the Football Association, UEFA (the Union of European Football Associations) and Sheffield Wednesday FC stage Group D matches at Hillsborough. The unit assists with many aspects of sports events; here is a summary:

- individual sports-related issues
- accommodation
- accreditation
- broadcasting and the media
- catering
- civic support
- event planning
- financial management
- fundraising
- marketing
- protocol
- publicity and promotion
- security and policing
- sponsorship
- transport and communications
- travel

For more information about staging a major sporting event in Sheffield, contact Martin Morton of the Sheffield Events Unit.

The events business and current position

Major sports events have a national dimension and an international dimension. Risk and uncertainty exist in both dimensions over performance quality and levels of spectator support.

In the international dimension there is a shifting balance of power affecting the decision-making process surrounding events allocation. The United Kingdom's position in world sport is declining and is currently causing concern to the Sports Council along with other national sports organisations and any cities that invest in international sporting facilities. Senior representatives of sport in the United Kingdom once held key positions within international sports federations. It is my feeling that the current lack of UK representation at this level has affected and will continue to affect ability of UK cities to attract international sporting events.

The sports events market is complicated by the range of organisations that now have an interest and involvement. These organisations can include national and international governing bodies, broadcast organisations, companies involved with sports sponsorship, sports marketing, sports management and sports technology (i.e. companies involved with timing, scoring and results services).

It is generally recognised that demand for events is initially a result of facility provision; it is therefore supply led. Recreational demand is generally more complex than demand for products, but demand for sports events may be simpler than for other forms of recreational activity. Demand for events in general is expected to grow within the United Kingdom. As the market develops, it will see sport adjusting its competitive structure and organisational arrangements to meet the demands and expectations of its consumers, its sponsors, its broadcasters and possibly its venue providers.

The range of facilities in Sheffield and their suitability for certain types of events – aquatics at Ponds Forge, athletics at Don Valley Stadium, indoor sports at the Sheffield Arena – directs the way the city can be involved in the events business. Although the choice of events for these facilities is wide, few of them meet the city's objectives and have minimal risk and uncertainty.

Sheffield is now recognised as a centre for major sports events and stands alongside other established European and world locations. This fact is acknowledged by the Sports Council, national governing bodies of sport and event promoters, and it was one of the prime reasons that Sheffield was designated as Britain's first national city of sport in July 1995. The city has a major sports events programme with projections being pursued into the next millennium.

The ability to plan in this way is a result of the facility provision, the skills, experience and results achieved over the last six years. A possible exception is the negative publicity which surrounded the WSG. In spite of this, the city has gained a reputation for the quality of its events organisation, and event promoters, governing bodies, broadcasters and sponsors have all expressed a wish to return. Remember that individuals and organisations wish to be associated with the best and with success. Sheffield is enjoying this with its events programme and is able to maximise the effect of its limited events budget.

A strategy for national and international sporting events

The development of a strategy for national and international sporting events was essential in order to maximise the efficiency of the Sheffield Events Unit's operation. This strategy also provides direction and a sense of purpose, which facilitates improved coordination of the identified aims and objectives.

The establishment of these aims and objectives and the criteria by which events are measured were a prerequisite to strategy formulation. The basic premise behind hosting national and international sporting events is the raising of the city's profile (city marketing) and stimulation of the local economy through multiplier effects. It is now well acknowledged that national and international sporting events are an integral component of the city's overall economic regeneration process.

Aims

1. To change Sheffield's image nationally and to raise its profile on the international stage providing a focus for sport and leisure as part of the diversified economic base which the city has created and a means to attract inward investment by demonstrating that Made in Sheffield, albeit applied in another context, is as true as it has ever been, synonymous with quality and achievement.

2. To play an integral role in stimulating the local community to collaborate and participate in sport and therefore increase the usage of all sports facilities in Sheffield.

Objectives

1. To link with major governing bodies of sport and event promoters to emphasise Sheffield's potential as a major sports venue at the highest level.

2. To work closely with the Sports Council's newly formed Major Events Support Group, in ensuring a city-coordinated approach, in particular with respect to international events.

3. To encourage visitor development and the subsequent stimulus of overnight stayers on the local economy.

4. To maximise Sheffield's national and international visibility (city marketing) via television and other media coverage of its major sports events.

5. To develop opportunities for involving and providing for the sporting disabled.

6. To promote Relocation to Sheffield opportunities for sports organisations and governing bodies and emphasise the city's potential as a major base for associated activities (national squads, training, seminars, conferences, etc.). The Sports Sheffield project and Destination Sheffield are two mechanisms by which this can happen.

7. To capitalise and take full advantage of the availability of external funding to offset event costs both in planning stages and actual event operations.

8. To attempt to spread the burden and risk associated with event attraction to include all those who might benefit from events being staged in Sheffield.

9. To increase penetration of the existing events market and develop an extension of this market to a regional catchment area and to a broader cross-section of customer groups.

10. To dovetail into existing sports development and community recreation initiatives to maximise opportunity and ensure best use of available resources.

11. To exploit the opportunities for corporate hospitality as a way of generating income to offset event-staging costs.

12. To dovetail cultural and artistic opportunities into the programme so that sporting and cultural activity complement each other.

13. To deliver the event within the agreed budget.

The Sheffield way: a three-step process

Selection criteria for major sports events

1. Does the event offer opportunities for the continued development of links with governing bodies of sport, emphasising Sheffield's potential as a venue for their particular major events? (This is selective according to the facilities portfolio that has been developed in Sheffield.)

2. What are the financial implications and the nature of the deal with the governing body of the sport or the event promoter? This is a crucial factor. At this stage, involvement and input from sponsors may assist in the decision whether or not to press for a particular event.

3. With most events there is a level of risk and uncertainty. To assist the decision-making process, as much intelligence work as possible is carried out and the maximum amount of information is gathered. Past financial and statistical information is analysed. Potential income sources are weighed up against projected expenditure. The net cost to the city is then the subject of a cost-benefit analysis.

4. Despite the costs of staging major events, there are numerous economic benefits besides civic and community pride, national and international profile (city marketing) together with other forms of secondary income.

5. This spending in the city by visitors in turn boosts the local economy – hotels, shopping, local transport, etc. – and naturally assists in developing the city's events-led strategy. These economic benefits have to be evaluated on an individual event basis.

6. An assessment is made on the level of media exposure afforded by the event in terms of developing Sheffield's regional, national and international profile (city marketing), especially via television.

7. Find out how much external funding, is available from the Sports Council and any other sources.

8. Does the event promote relocation to Sheffield, create opportunities for sports organisations and governing bodies, and increase the city's potential as a major base for associated activities (training, seminars, conferences, etc.)?

9. What is the impact of the event in stimulating the local community to collaborate and participate in sport?

10. Is there a possible link with the development of centres of excellence and the appointment of sports-specific development officers?

11. What are the opportunities for involving and serving the sporting disabled? The WSG Our Year Too programme has continued and developed and now has charitable status.

12. What are the event's status and credibility? How is it perceived in the events market-place? Into which category does the event fall, i.e. calendar, participation, entertainment, hybrid or created event.

13. Can the city manage the operational implications of the event? What is the availability of suitably trained volunteers? Are there appropriate staff and resources?

14. Timing and scheduling should be critically analysed. Wherever possible, bid preparations and deadlines should be evaluated to see whether they are realistically achievable.

15. Does the event allow a quality service to be given to the customer and can it satisfy their demands and expectations?

16. An attempt should be made to quantify the added value of the event to the city. More quantifiable aspects can be assessed, such as length and scope of television coverage (city marketing) along with estimated viewing figures and the estimated number of overnight stays associated with the event.

Event evaluation

1. As a result of proactive research and investigation, or a governing body approach to Sheffield with a request to stage a particular event, a comprehensive evaluation is required to determine the potential of the event to satisfy the aims and achieve the objectives of Sheffield's major sports events programme.

2. There needs to be consultation with the Sports Council's Major Events Support Group. The secretary of state has announced that the Lottery Sports Fund can now be used to assist the revenue costs of staging major sport events. The English Football Association have already consulted the prime minister and the secretary of state about available support for a bid to stage the FIFA World Cup in the year 2006.

3. Informal discussion and communication take place within the city's sports events, sports development and community recreation sections.

4. Facility management representatives are consulted about the availability of venues and to obtain an estimate of costs.

5. Accommodation requirements are checked with Destination Sheffield (the city's visitor and conference bureau) and prices are obtained, where appropriate. If it is concluded that the city cannot satisfy the required accommodation specification, all potential accommodation providers will be consulted as to their future development plans. And if an event promoter or sports governing body is particularly keen on price, and the success or otherwise of the event being attracted is at stake, the accommodation providers should be made aware of this before being asked to quote.

6. An evaluation panel is formed as follows:
   - principal events officer
   - operations manager (events)
   - sports development officer and/or sports-specific development officer
   - facility representative

7. The evaluation panel will evaluate the event against the event selection criteria, giving a more objective decision on whether or not to pursue the event.

8. Large-scale events like the World Masters Swimming Championships include discussions and consultation with other city council departments, where specialist expertise is available, e.g. the city treasury and the legal and administration department.

Operational management

1. At this stage a contract or an agreement in writing between the city council and the governing body or promoter should be finalised, clearly setting out the division of responsibilities and the level of financial commitment.

2. The agreement procedure should then be repeated for all other agencies involved in the proposed event. This clear division of responsibilities is crucial and should

include other city council departments, including direct service and direct labour organisations.

3. On the basis of being awarded the event, and in consultation with the sports governing body, the evaluation panel will then formulate and recommend the most appropriate event-organising structure to suit the nature or size of the event.

4. At this stage the roles of individuals within the Sheffield Events Unit can be identified and managed accordingly.

5. Likewise, the role of other individuals and groups involved in the event should be identified, including those of the sports governing body or the promoter along with other city council departments and other partners.

6. Contact has to be made with a local representative of the sport featured in the event. The timing and contact will vary according to the scale of the event.

How to bid for international sporting events

For international sporting events it is the host federation or national governing body that formally makes a bid to its international federation to secure an event. Once the event is secured and there is a contractual agreement with the international federation, then the host federation will have to enter into a contract with its chosen host city.

It is the decision of the host federation to select the prospective venue. It may wish to select a venue before bidding to the international federation, thereby confirming first an agreed level of support from that particular host city.

In the case of the 1996 European Football Championships in England, the Football Association received 'in principle' support from central government before bidding to UEFA to stage the event. However, it did not consult the local authorities within the host cities until after the event had been secured. This caused concern for those authorities, who were likely to incur costs if matches were staged in their cities. These costs included such things as traffic management and additional cleaning. There was also an expectation that host cities would develop a programme of sporting and cultural festivals.

Some international federations award sporting events to the actual country of the national federation and allow the national federation to select the most suitable host city after the award has been made. Prospective bidding cities should beware of this process. On previous occasions in England, national governing bodies of sport have been known to secure European and World Championship events on the understanding that they would take place in a particular city, only for the national governing body to choose another city at a later date.

Sheffield has enjoyed the support of many organisations when bidding for international sporting events. The two city universities, local hotels and restaurants, Destination Sheffield (the city's visitor and conference bureau), the Sheffield Chambers of Commerce and Trade and many local businesses have all at some stage provided cash or support in kind. In addition, the British Tourist Authority has been extremely supportive of bids that could result in large numbers of people visiting the United Kingdom from abroad (city marketing). On many occasions it has contributed significantly to the marketing and promotion of international bids.

The national process of bidding for international sporting events used to be unstructured and uncoordinated. However, the introduction of the Sports Council's Major Events Support Group is an initiative that has been welcomed by Sheffield and will lead to a much more cohesive and objective strategy for the staging of international sporting events in the United Kingdom.

Financing of bids and events

The costs of bidding and staging international sporting events can often be a financial burden to the host city. Many governing bodies of sport require the prospective host city to fund the bid process and underwrite the total cost of the event. And many governing bodies of sport have little or no experience in event bidding and staging and they are unaware of the financial and organisational implications associated with staging international events.

In essence, UK cities such as Sheffield, Birmingham and Glasgow have been subsidising sport. By the introduction of revenue support from the Lottery Sports Fund, the UK government has demonstrated it is keen to raise the profile of UK sport overseas, offering financial assistance to those cities who have made the investment in high-quality spectator facilities.

Programme monitoring and evaluation

In order to measure the effectiveness of this type of programme, it is essential to incorporate a mechanism for monitoring and evaluation. The feedback from this mechanism can illustrate the effectiveness of the city-marketing strategy. Success can usually be measured by the quantifiable and tangible benefits to the city. But it is harder to measure image or marketing gains. As part of our post-event evaluation, these benefits are logged and we can measure them against our expectations for that particular event. This post-event process can vary from some basic in-house analysis to a more complex external study or commission, as for the World Masters Swimming Championships and Euro '96.

The significance behind hosting national and international sporting events is their role in city marketing. Equally important to these marketing gains is the way events stimulate the local economy through multiplier effects. There is worldwide acknowledgement that these events can contribute significantly to a city's overall economic regeneration plan. Secondary spending in the city by participants, spectators, officials and other visitors, boosts the local economy. Hotels, restaurants, pubs and clubs, shopping and local transport all benefit, helping to develop the events-led strategy, as pioneered by Sheffield.

Despite the associated costs of staging major sports events, through its programme of monitoring and evaluation, Sheffield has recorded an uplift in civic and community pride (particularly during the actual events), national and international profile (city marketing) as well as many economic benefits from secondary spending. This kind of programme is also of great benefit to the local sports community, providing opportunities for active and passive participation. Here are some of the remarkable statistics of what has been achieved in Sheffield through the programme of major sports events since 1990:

- Designation as Britain's first national city of sport.
- It has hosted 320 national and international sporting events, including 39 single-sport events.
- A total of 17 different sporting venues have been used, public and private sector.
- It has hosted 13 World and 9 European Championships in six years.
- World and European Championships have involved over one million people as participants, spectators or officials.
- It is estimated that over £45 million has been spent in the local economy, directly attributable to this programme. This equates to a very favourable return on investment for the city council. For each £1 spent on the programme, £37.50 is ploughed back into the local economy.

Media profile and city marketing through television broadcasting and advertising at prime time is a business cost that would prove prohibitive outside a programme of national and international events.

● Of the 320 events hosted by Sheffield, 88 have received national or international television coverage. Many others have been covered regionally.

● The McDonalds Games IAAF Permit meeting held at the Don Valley Stadium in 1996 received two hours of prime-time coverage on national television and was watched by over 5.3 million viewers. Moreover, the pictures were transmitted by Eurosport via satellite to twenty European countries with an estimated viewing audience of over 20 million. It is estimated that the television coverage received by the city as a result of staging these events has a value in the region of £90 million.

Self-assessment questions

1. From an event you have been involved in or attended, identify the general aim and up to five SMART objectives. Go on to examine four of the key questions, issues or items which would have to be considered.

2. Make up your own list of twenty key factors in following the idea of holding a village fete successfully.

3. Consider an agency – a local authority, private company or voluntary organisation – and suggest what part events do play or could play in their overall strategic plan.

Chapter Two

Management

According to an anonymous saying:

Management is the art of getting other people to do all the work.

Good management is the key to successful event organisation. Whether the event is local or international, the effective implementation of sound organisational and individual management principles and practices is crucial to effectiveness. Dictionary definitions of *management* include words like these: conducting, directing, controlling, leading, handling, helping and training. Management is about getting things done, through effective people and efficient processes.

The famous management writer Peter F. Drucker defines a manager as 'one who has the task of creating a true whole that is larger than the sum of its parts, a productive entity that turns out more than the sum of the resources put into it'. This again emphasises that unity of purpose is what good management aims for, earlier identified as vital to any good event. At the outset of any event, we should make unity of purpose one of our key objectives. And in obtaining this unity, through good management, a number of central concepts have to be considered and employed.

In studying management it is normal to examine its principles or functions. There is no definitive list – different authors prefer different aspects or emphases – so it is vital to look more closely at the principles most relevant to organising events, bearing in mind that different people may have different words for the same concepts and perhaps different views about them. For events, the important factor is their practical implementation, although theoretical study will aid good practice.

The main functions of management

Here are the main functions of management. Chapter 3 covers organising and communicating, so they are not considered in this section.

- organising
- planning
- motivating
- communicating
- creating
- controlling
- problem solving

Creating

Creating is the first step in the planning process. A manager needs to provide the initiative by presenting the hypothesis which, through a feasibility study, can be put to the test. After all, someone has to come up with the original idea for the event. Innovative thinking skills will help to create a workable concept, an interesting event based on the client's needs, and very important novel ways of funding the project. It is equally important for the manager to be able to apply free thinking to the implementation of an event. A good event manager will also be able to link together suitable ideas or tasks to achieve the identified goals in an innovative and encouraging way. Always remember that creativity must be set in the proper context, linked to finance and resources. Creativity without a sound base is unreal and equals disaster.

Problem solving

Problems are only opportunities in work clothes.

(Henry J. Kaiser)

Problem solving is an essential skill for getting action in events. This is absolutely vital to those working on events, as anyone with experience will testify. Problems will always arise and it needs a positive, innovative thinker to solve them. Imaginative and lateral thinking may be very helpful in facing up to difficulties and finding solutions. Problem solving has several stages:

1. Obtain the facts.
2. Specify the objectives.
3. Identify the problem.
4. Formulate alternative solutions.
5. Select the best solution.
6. Put the selected solution into practice.
7. Continue making observations to ensure the chosen solution works.
8. Select a new solution or adjust any corrective action; or go back to step 1.

Problem solving is closely linked to crisis management; it is the ability to solve problems before they become crises. Concentrate on developing personal skills, strength and analytical ability to disentangle any problem faced. It is vital to improve these analytical skills by practising the segmentation of issues into their relevant parts. Try to become systematic in approaching problems, so as not to overlook important details, especially under pressure. Equally it is important to take on an uncomplicated and innovative attitude to problems. An overly complex approach will only cloud the issue and suggest old ideas; it will seldom produce a novel or appropriate solution.

Motivating

Keeping staff motivated and interested is always important in any demanding work situation, although in events there is often the benefit that many are already involved because of their commitment. But this should never be taken for granted and a special effort is needed to keep motivation high, especially because events invariably demand an extraordinary dedication from everyone involved.

The first essential is a clear understanding of the aims and objectives of the event by all concerned; this achieves unity of purpose and keeps the end target in everyone's mind. The atmosphere of the event must be realistic, open and honest from beginning to end, and staff must be kept informed at all times. Financial difficulties or any other problems must be communicated to staff as they occur, because undue secrecy can be very demotivating.

In return for the often heavy work demands put on those involved in events, tangible rewards may be minimal. Job satisfaction and pleasure in a successful conclusion is probably the largest reward. For some this can be adequate, but for others it is not so important; bear this in mind when making demands on staff. Overtime payments may be difficult but, if possible, they are worthwhile in assisting staff interest. Money, though, does not motivate everyone (or indeed many) involved in leisure events.

It is absolutely vital for an event leader to try to understand what motivates their staff or volunteers and do all they can to meet their individual and group needs. In particular, it is essential to recognise the role played by individuals in an event structure; some form of public recognition may be a great motivation in a local event. It may be possible to give staff a uniform to help create an identity and coordinate effort. Any little perk, like the use of a courtesy car, free meals, or the legendary T-shirt may well help to motivate people and increase their commitment; little rewards go a long way.

The demands of an event are usually beyond the norm, so any motivation will have to be exceptional as well. Remember that getting people to do what you want is manipulation not motivation; the aim is to get them to want what you want.

Controlling

From the start, it must be clear that control does not mean anything sinister or imply the manipulation of individuals; it is about monitoring the performance of systems and resources. Control is the management function that checks to see if what is supposed to happen is happening, or going to happen. This is a crucial part of event management because it is necessary for things to actually happen, not just promised to happen.

In the planning stages of an event, control systems must be established to check that objectives are accomplished within the prescribed timescale. Effective control has four stages:

1. Plan what you intend to do.
2. Measure what has been done.
3. Compare achievements with the blueprint.
4. Take action to correct anything that is not as it should be.

In practical terms, control can be exerted in several ways:

- *Financial checks* ensure that expenditure is incurred as and when expected; this is essential.
- *At least two people know* that critical tasks have been achieved.
- *Modern technology* monitors actual achievement.
- *Comprehensive reporting and communication systems* detect all unaccomplished tasks.
- *Flexible control* adapts to changing circumstances and allows enough time to adapt easily.
- *Regular reporting* exists for all groups and individuals.

While delegating and encouraging everyone to do their bit, it is vital to implement systems to ensure everything is done. Proper control will ensure a proper end result.

Planning

The wise man looks ahead.

(Proverb)

It is always a little dangerous to select one management function as more important than another, but in terms of event organisation, it would be quite legitimate to select planning as the prime factor in achieving success. Careful planning is absolutely vital to good events; things don't just happen or appear by accident, they are produced by effective planning and thought.

Planning is the process of setting goals and deciding on the best approach to achieve them. Time spent in careful planning is time well spent; it will be repaid later on because it will help to eliminate wasteful, misdirected effort. Three types of plan should be produced for an event:

- *Strategic plans* direct an organisation towards its overall objectives, taking account of major influences: political, environmental, economic, etc.
- *Specific plans* are designed to achieve specific objectives, e.g. budget estimates, resource production and promotion plans.
- *Administrative, organisational and structural plans* explain how the objectives will be achieved.

Planning is so valuable because it reduces uncertainty, focuses attention on goals, produces unity of purpose, makes for efficient operation and ensures appropriate control systems are established.

Stages in event planning

1. Determine the event vision and aims.
2. Formulate a policy; adopt the vision and examine its consequences.
3. Carry out a feasibility study and make key decisions.
4. Set the SMART objectives.
5. Identify the resources and check their availability.
6. Identify the tasks to be undertaken.
7. Define the organisational structure and identify the roles.
8. Select the personnel.
9. Choose an appropriate communication structure.
10. Draw up a budget.
11. Make detailed plans and specify the timescale; work backwards from the event itself.
12. Plan any meetings and choose the control systems.
13. Plan the event implementation, its presentation, preparation, closure and clearing.
14. Finalise the accounts; evaluate whether the aims and objectives were achieved, and record any modifications to consider when organising future events.

As suggested at stage 11 of this planning process, it will be necessary to set down a detailed timescale. This is vital because an event is totally time dependent; only tasks completed within the time available can make the event a success, and any delay can be fatal.

Figure 2.1
Key tasks and
their timescales

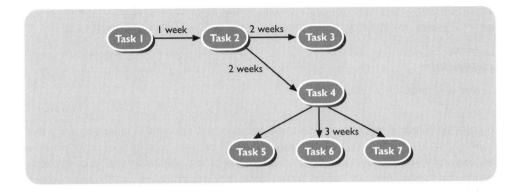

The engineering and construction industries use critical path analysis to determine project progress, and although it can be rather elaborate for some situations, it is advisable to use some type of diagram at stage 11 (Fig. 2.1). It should be designed to suit each specific event, and will be a major benefit to the planning and monitoring process. For bigger events there could even be a planning chart for each working group, devised by themselves and giving their key dates. But chart or no chart, the planning must be thorough, careful and detailed. Only a well-planned event will be a good event. Remember, failure to plan is planning to fail!

Other management concepts

Several other concepts identified in management are particularly relevant to event management and its peculiar stresses and strains. So before moving on to look at some of the personal management skills, we consider decision making, team building, delegation, leadership, staff appraisal and training, authority, responsibility of power, crisis management and problem solving.

Decision making

He who hesitates is lost.

(Proverb)

Decision making is an integral part of management in any kind of organisation. It is impossible to give a formula for how to approach this, but some general principles should be applied, and in a pressured situation it is often advisable to follow them.

Decision making in events takes place at several levels: individual, group and organisational. At whatever level, decision making involves the assessment and implementation of possible strategies, considering flexibility, the individual's attitude to risk and the organisation's response to it. In an event, as the end result will effect everyone, it is normally better to use 'democratic' decision making to try to involve as many people as possible. It is also sensible to use the collective knowledge of the group to help reach the correct decision, and to help generate unity of purpose so that agreed decisions contribute to the joint ownership of the project.

Team building

Getting results through people is a skill that cannot be learned in the classroom.

(J. Paul Getty)

To some extent, this management skill is indefinable and concerns psychological aspects such as morale, camaraderie and personality traits. Although its definition may be difficult, it is essential that any event manager makes a real effort to build his or her team. Unity of purpose and an atmosphere of cooperation are essential to achieve success in the often pressured world of event management.

Recognition of an organisation's formal and informal aspects will aid teamwork and allow both aspects to be promoted. Informal meetings should be encouraged to help build relationships and promote joint understandings, and so should clear structures and chains of command, which help to avoid confusion and conflict. Formal training, informal socialising, group decision making and full staff involvement at all stages will help to build an effective team. This is very important to events of all sizes, with volunteers as well as paid staff; it may even be essential in the voluntary sector.

Delegation

What is worth doing is worth the trouble of asking somebody to do it.

(Ambrose Bierce)

Delegation is a key management activity and is crucial to the success of any event. It is not abdication of power, it means giving people something to do which they are capable of achieving. Bear in mind that the coordinator will still carry the can for failure, if failure is the result. It is important to do this in the right way, by planned delegation not just a random allocation of tasks. Ask yourself what can be delegated and what benefits there would be in somebody else doing any particular job. It may be that jobs will initially take a little longer when delegated, perhaps even the quality may be lower, but the old saying is very true of events: 1% of 100 people is better than 100% of one person. It achieves more in the long term.

Remember that delegation is not dumping, or an opportunity to offload all the boring or difficult tasks. Delegation is designed to get success through maximising efficiency, using everyone's time, expertise and effort to the best purpose. It is important to select tasks that will provide individuals with some challenge and sense of achievement when they are completed, not just menial tasks the team leader doesn't want to do. Clear direction must be given, tasks delegated must not be vague or require people to spend lots of time and effort seeking clarification.

Be aware of the capacity and willingness of the individual or group to handle the task being delegated. Delegate to those who are competent and likely to be capable of achieving the task (with coaching and training). Always encourage delegation as far down the organisation as possible. Commitment and motivation come through delegation and the opportunity to achieve real tasks. Generally speaking, people will rise to real challenges.

Give precise instructions of what you want to be achieved, including what, by when and to what standard. But give direction on how this is to be done. Ensure that arrangements for reporting progress and seeking help are clearly understood. Let other people that will be affected by delegation know what is happening. During the delegation process, ask for progress reports and check them regularly. This shows that the leader is still interested.

It is also necessary to give positive feedback in a constructive way to help the person achieve the task. In an event of any significant size, the central leader will not be able to achieve everything themselves, so effective delegation will be essential.

Leadership

Leadership is an inter-personal influence exercised in situations and directed through the communication process towards the attainment of a specified goal or goals.

(Tannenbaum and Massarik)

It is impossible to overemphasise the crucial need for an effective, charismatic leader for any successful event. The way must be charted and the lead taken; success is impossible without a captain and a rudderless event will flounder.

Similar to beauty, good leadership is in the eye of the beholder, but here are some of the qualities required for event management:

- approachable
- decisive
- hard working
- flexible
- knowledgeable
- innovative
- firm but fair
- diplomatic
- charismatic
- imaginative
- understanding
- democratic style
- resourceful
- motivating
- enthusiastic
- perceptive
- analytical
- well organised
- blessed with a sense of humour
- financially aware
- good at listening
- communicative
- opportunist
- questioning
- inspirational

Taken together, they add up to Superman or Superwoman.

As events can range from formal to informal, the leader needs to vary from authoritarian to friendly as the occasion demands. It is very much a case of leading by example, demonstrating commitment and a sense of purpose then hoping that others will follow.

The real leader has no need to lead. He is content to point the way.

(Henry Miller)

It may be necessary on some occasions to take an assertive line with fellow workers, but more often encouragement through force of personality and example will be the order of the day. An effective leader will show the staff they care, tell them exactly what is required, share the overall event experience, and reward or rebuke workers as required. The style and quality of the leader will be a deciding factor in the success of any event.

The style of leadership can vary on a continuum from laissez-faire to dictatorial, with a number of stages in between.

Dictator ◆──▶ Authoritarian ◆──▶ Democratic ◆──▶ Consensus ◆──▶ Laissez-faire

The only style which is totally inappropriate to events is laissez-faire (leave to do) because, with nobody at the helm, an event would hit the rocks, or at the very least it

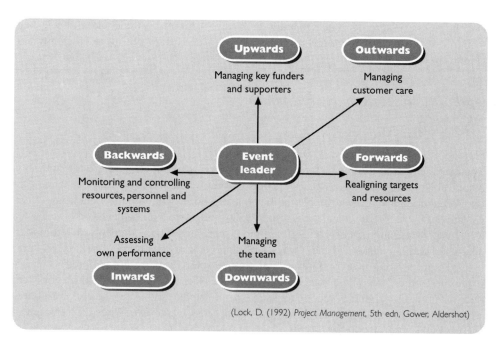

Figure 2.2
An event leader
must look around

(Lock, D. (1992) *Project Management*, 5th edn, Gower, Aldershot)

would lack direction. And a complete dictator would be equally unacceptable, especially where volunteers were involved. A dogmatic approach will be ineffective in most event situations and will often cause problems rather than achieve progress.

In essence, the style of the leader has to match the situation, but it will usually allow for a significant contribution by others. Those who are excluded from decision making may also feel excluded from achieving the aims of the event, and they are not likely to follow any leader who does not involve them. A positive but democratic and pragmatic approach to leadership is normally the way to retain a degree of control alongside unity of purpose. The key leader will also be required to provide vision, direction and an awareness of the external environment to ensure success. They should look around them and keep the event on track (Fig. 2.2).

Staff appraisal and training

Due to the transitory nature of events, the area of personnel development is often ignored. This is very wrong, as many of the special people and skills required will need to be cultured rather than just found. Staff appraisal may be difficult, due to a limited timescale, but any comments to staff on their performance, strengths and weaknesses will enhance their efforts. People appreciate constructive guidance rather than just being left to flounder under pressure.

Time must be made for staff training which will prove of considerable benefit to the whole process. It is always beneficial to have highly skilled, knowledgeable staff, whether voluntary or paid. There are two types of training for event staff:

● *Desirable training* improves personal skills like decision making or creativity.

● *Essential training* ensures personnel are aware of legal requirements, e.g. under health and safety legislation, and can perform routine word processing and computing tasks

Despite time pressure, as much training as possible should be undertaken; it will help to improve the quality of the event and allow it to be carried out more efficiently and effectively.

Authority, responsibility and power

Knowledge is power.

(Francis Bacon)

The management and the structure of any event must make it clear where the authority, responsibility and power lie. These concepts are important and are a vital part of delegation; remember, it's not just the blame that's delegated! It will be more beneficial, effective and enjoyable for staff if authority, responsibility and power can be devolved or delegated as far as possible and practicable. Staff are more motivated if they are really able to undertake and complete tasks without always reporting back or seeking permission.

It is important that everyone knows where they stand, and are not tempted to underplay or indeed overstep their role, especially in areas like financial expenditure. For every decision and every spend, someone must take responsibility and everyone else must know who it is. Communication is a key part of this process; make clear lines of communication and where responsibility lies.

Crisis management

You're either part of the solution or part of the problem.

(Eldridge Cleaver)

It is hard to imagine an event without some sort of crisis or to envisage such firefighting skills as being unnecessary for any event organiser. As Kipling said, 'If you can keep your head when all about you are losing theirs and blaming it on you.' The golden rule for any problem is don't panic, easy to say but difficult to do. In events, one can often be judged by one's reaction to any crisis when it arises. The ability to handle such situations is arguably the key skill for senior staff in event management; a good manager faces crises and handles them calmly and effectively.

By careful preplanning and forethought, a good organiser should aim to avoid as many crises as possible. In addition, as part of the same process, the staff can be prepared for appropriate action when a crisis does arise, by laying down clear contingency plans. It is colloquially known as Sod's law: if you don't plan for a disaster, it's bound to happen; if you do, it almost certainly won't! Allied to good staff training, foresight anticipates problems and makes them easier to handle. Well-trained staff are likely to cause fewer crises and will also be better able to handle any that occur. A number of steps are essential for resolving any crisis:

1. Coolly analyse the situation – as coolly as possible!
2. Re-examine the objectives.
3. Examine the possibilities.
4. Consider the consequences of various solutions.
5. Select the best (least damaging) option.
6. Implement the appropriate action.
7. Continue monitoring to avoid repetition.

For crisis management, a team analysis and attack will be more successful. In a people business, individuals can cause problems, but working as part of a group, they can also solve them.

Managing people, meetings and time

Management is not just about concepts or results, it is about people. The personality and management style of any leader is going to have a profound effect on how an event turns out. The democratic and charismatic leader will generally achieve more with volunteers than the autocrat, who may succeed with paid staff. The pressure of events needs everyone to work willingly and not be pressured.

The variables that influence the best choice of approach, if there is a best choice, depend on many things: venue, finance, commitment, expectations, etc. A good event manager will try to balance all factors and adjust their leadership style accordingly. The list of management functions could be long, too long for this text, but here are some that may need to be considered in certain situations:

- consulting
- inspiring
- anticipating
- informing
- analysing

- resolving
- budgeting
- recruiting
- supervising
- reviewing

Personal management

The first requirement in effective management is managing yourself. When you manage yourself well, you are in a better position to achieve, to be effective and to work in cooperation with others. There are several main considerations to managing yourself in an events situation:

- Know yourself as a manager; understand how you operate and how you are perceived by others.
- Have clear objectives and identify the right priorities.
- Ensure efficient personal organisation.
- Be clear about personal roles and responsibilities, and know your place within the organisation.

The first two of these items are difficult to quantify. Personal analysis is always difficult, but a good manager should take time for genuine personal reflection. To manage others effectively and efficiently, you need to understand how you tackle jobs that you find hard. Training in, and study of, the management process and leadership styles will help you in measuring your personal skills against the ideal. Your own experience and track record will also be a guide to your strengths and weaknesses. Time spent on personal self-analysis will be time well spent.

Objectives and priorities may vary in the general sense, but for events they are set by the aim, objectives and timescale of the particular project. Similarly, roles and responsibilities need to be clarified and agreed for each event, and this action will greatly assist both personal and organisational operation. Most of us can make massive improvements in our personal efficiency. There are many good publications on self-organisation, and the dedicated event organiser could do well to study them. Enhancing certain skills will improve behaviour management and increase work performance.

EVENT ORGANISERS

Must try to be	Develop the ability to	Try to remain
responsible	keep healthy	enthusiastic
listening	say no	approachable
efficient	think things through	positive
organised	prioritise	skilled
an example	research	responsive
logical	record	
a facilitator		

Time management

The best preparation for good work tomorrow is to do good work today.
(Elbert Hubbard)

It is inevitable that in all stages of event planning, preparation and implementation, time will seem to be extremely limited. As the principles of general management apply to events, so too do those of time management; they really do play a central role in the event management situation.

Good time management is crucial during the last few weeks and days before any event, and throughout the event itself. Time will become more limited; there may be many tight deadlines, and problems can arise which will affect them. Although one tries to prepare for all contingencies, good time management leaves time available to deal with crises. Planning time must be found if events are going to be well managed and organised. Effective time management will mean that you become better at:

- organising
- planning
- delegating
- controlling stress

To get to this happy situation, several measures can be taken. First of all, the following time wasters should be avoided. Some of them are brought on yourself and some are engendered by other people:

- procrastination
- an untidy desk
- poor paperwork control
- inefficient planning
- ineffective delegation
- inability to say no
- excessive control
- inability to terminate visits, especially unsolicited visits
- poor organisation
- lengthy, ineffective meetings
- interruptions (telephone)
- interruptions (physical)
- poor communication
- unnecessary delays
- underskilled staff
- mistakes by others

Elimination of time wasters will leave more time available for the real work on the event. But there are also some positive steps to increase the time available:

- Once in a while, analyse how you spend your time; do you use it effectively? Time spent on thinking and planning is not time wasted.

- Learn how to manage paper. Don't write things unnecessarily. It takes time to write and time to read.

- Use memos only to pass on information. It is better to discuss contentious issues or pass on criticism.

- When you write, get it right. Written work gives an impression, be succinct and accurate.

- Keep distribution and copy lists to a minimum, and take your name off unnecessary distribution lists.

- Keep a chronological file of all correspondence, reduce the number of subject files and make things easier to find.

- Keep filing to a minimum, use central or shared files wherever possible and purge historic files ruthlessly.

- Sort out your mail into urgent, non-urgent and interesting. Process it in that order. Try to process paper only once.

- Prioritise your phone calls. Make the short ones first.

- Get some quiet 'doing and thinking' time reserved in your diary.

- During an event, or the sometimes frenetic lead-up, constantly carry a Dictaphone or notepad, instantly recording points to be remembered or acted upon. Points which flash into the mind can be recorded and dealt with at an appropriate time, without clouding any current considerations or discussions.

- Create a 'to do' list. Having noted all the tasks that face us, the next step is to grade them A, B or C. Aim to get all the A's done, then the B's and then the C's. By the end of the day, the list will be a mess – some items scored, others added, etc. – but just carry it on to the next day. Don't be tempted simply to knock off the trivia; try to do some key tasks too.

Careful preplanning is absolutely vital, as in many other areas of event management.

Managing meetings

Meetings are indispensable when you don't want to do anything

(J.K. Galbraith)

Many have written whole books on this topic alone. When setting up any event, a number of meetings will inevitably be required. To maximise their effectiveness, be aware of some basic principles for organising them:

1. Hold meetings only when they are required.
2. Involve only those people who can contribute and will benefit from being present.
3. Keep meetings brief and to the point.
4. Have a detailed agenda and a timetable for it.
5. Be properly prepared for your role in the meeting.
6. Have clear objectives for the meeting.
7. Keep accurate minutes or notes of what happens.
8. Have a series of actions listed to be taken after the meeting.

9. Don't allow individuals or the meeting to ramble.

10. Make positive not negative contributions.

11. Set a time limit for the meeting.

12. Hold only meetings that produce action.

Following these guidelines will help to make meetings more bearable, and more worthwhile. A leisure event is like any other project or any other business; it needs to be well managed. By adhering to the principles identified, it will be possible to produce a successful event.

Self-assessment questions

1. It is always difficult to prioritise management functions, but now try. Think of a practical event situation, identify the five most important management functions and justify your choice of each.

2. You are to act as the key event organiser for next year's village fete in Ambridge. Which particular leadership skills do you think you will have to portray and why?

3. Consider how you organise your personal life currently, and drawing on the sections on personal time and meeting management, identify ways in which you could become more effective.

Chapter Three

Organisation and Communication

These two concepts have been given a separate chapter because they are so important. Organisation and communication are central to the event management process, so they should be studied at length by the project practitioner or student.

Organisation

Organising may be considered as

> the determining of the special activities to be accomplished towards the end objectives; the gathering of these activities into relevant structures; and the allocation of the achievement of objectives, through these activities, to the appropriate groups or individuals.

Managers need to understand organisations. Organisations provide the framework within which individuals can cooperate to achieve what they could not achieve on their own. Organisation is the way that ideals and aims are turned into reality. Laying down a structure, defining who does what, will be a key step to achieving an event.

Organisation should bring about synergy. Synergy should really make one plus one equal three; in other words, the whole is greater than the sum of its parts:

Our
Regime
Gets
Action
Necessary
Inside
Structures
Appropriate
To
Individuals and
Organisation
Now

Every organisation has a reason for its existence, very often several reasons; but in the case of events there is one prime objective: to offer a quality service that carries off the event successfully, thereby satisfying the needs of all event customers.

Remember that organisational structures involve people; people are the focus. Developing working relationships will be of crucial importance, alongside the definition of working roles, tasks to be achieved and the structure to be used. The focus of any organisation must be on achieving the necessary action through its personnel. The chosen organisational system will need to be flexible, so it can cope with the changing circumstances that often arise during events, especially the larger ones. There are several steps in choosing an organisational structure for an event:

1. Define the aims and objectives of the project.
2. Analyse the background situation in which the event has to be achieved (external and internal environmental audit).
3. List all the tasks to be undertaken.
4. Group together all related tasks.
5. Establish links between these groups of tasks.
6. Establish an understanding of respective roles for all those involved.
7. Identify possible communication lines between various groups.

Many organisations possess a number of features that affect how they function. One of them is the coexistence of formal and informal structures, both fundamental to relationships. Communication will not be just along preset lines, so care must be taken to ensure that formal and informal structures do not conflict with each other. An effective informal structure is especially important when dealing with voluntary event staff; the approach must be professional, but the atmosphere may need to be more relaxed. The structure of an organisation is determined by the functions it performs to achieve the event. Any structure should be designed to meet these functions in a manner as appropriate and efficient as possible.

Having decided on the organisational layout, the various tasks have to be carefully allocated to the relevant section; nothing should be left unassigned. The size of the structure will depend on the level, complexity and exact nature of the event, but do not make it unnecessarily complicated. It is equally important to ensure that everyone involved knows who they are in charge of, or subordinate to; what are their exact duties; and where is their place within the structure.

The structure may be formalised in a chart, but this should not suggest it is set in stone, incapable of being modified. A large event may require quite a detailed chart to display the structure clearly; any confusion could be damaging. The number of possible structures is almost infinite; it is hard to give general guidelines on choosing a structure, but past experience on other events may give a good indication. Figures 3.1 and 3.2 illustrate a few possibilities, and some examples are given later in the book.

After establishing the overall structure to achieve the event, specify the detailed remits for each individual or group involved (Fig. 3.3). Explain exactly what each is responsible for doing, and make clear how it relates to others. This process of devising and allocating tasks will be needed for every organising group, as well as each and every subcommittee and each member of staff (paid or voluntary). No one should be involved without a specific job remit, coupled with a clear understanding of what everyone else is doing. *Everyone* should be in possession of a precise job remit, from the chair of the executive group to the humblest worker.

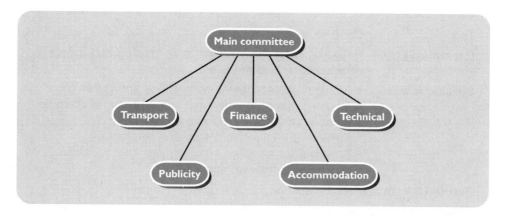

Figure 3.1
A simple organisational structure. Under each heading there may be a small committee or just an individual who feeds into the main committee, or who sits on it

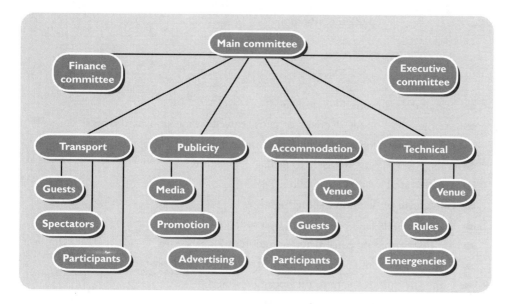

Figure 3.2
A more complex organisational structure. An even more complex structure, required only for major events, is shown on p. 134

The organisational structure, relationship diagram and job description, should combine to answer the following questions for each individual or group:

- What is my position?
- What are my tasks?
- What is my role?
- To whom am I accountable?
- What are my objectives?
- Who is accountable to me?

An organisation checklist

Having established the organisational structure, it is advisable to check the end result against a few questions:

- Are all duties and responsibilities correctly identified?
- Is the work divided appropriately?

Figure 3.3

A job remit

Title	Car park supervisor
General role	Responsible for the safe entrance, parking and exit of all vehicles coming to the event.
Specific duties	• Arranging appropriate parking space and layout. • Ensuring ease of entrance and exit for all vehicles: 2 hours for entrance, 30 minutes for exit. • Parking all vehicles in a safe and secure way. • Providing for all special groups, e.g. VIPs, disabled. • Liaising with relevant agencies.
Responsible to	Venue manager
Responsible for	Six stewards
Liaison with	Police Traffic wardens Roads dept. Fire brigade VIP coordinator

- Are all efforts properly coordinated?
- Are there any undue overlaps or gaps between allocations and work?
- Are activities allocated to individuals or groups with appropriate skills?
- Is the work allocated wisely to facilitate workflow?
- Are allocated tasks closely linked?
- Is the level of decision making right?
- Do individuals take orders from two sources?
- Are there properly constructed communication systems?
- Is proper account taken of individual and group relationships?
- Is the structure relevant to the specific event?
- Will the structure achieve a successful outcome for the event?
- Does everyone involved have a detailed job specification?
- Is everyone aware of organisational and communication structures?

The organisational structure for events should cover planning, developing, working relationships and ways to achieve objectives. The structure should cover chains of command, span of control and areas of delegated responsibility. It should be relevant, effective and designed specifically for each event.

Coordination

A structure may be appropriate and people may do work, but little will be achieved unless their efforts are coordinated. Coordination is crucial to successful organisation and management. It follows from the division of labour in the previous section, so that tasks can be allocated and achieved. All organisations need coordinating mechanisms like clearly defined status and work roles, as well as informal communication and detailed committee remits. More sophisticated mechanisms, like project teams and coordinators, are more expensive but they may be helpful for major events, so that everyone knows what everyone else is doing.

In general terms, coordination comes from having a shared goal and common objectives, within an appropriate culture and structure. Everyone must work hard continually in an effort to preserve this unity of purpose, so vital to cohesive and successful events of all sizes. If this unity of purpose is present and preserved, and all the organisation, planning, delegation and control systems are correctly selected and operating, then coordination should follow quite naturally.

Communication

Effective communication leads to good coordination, hence an efficient organisation. Internal and external communication are vital to successful event management in many ways and at every level, among individuals and between organisations. Communication may be defined as 'the giving, receiving or exchange of information, so that the material communicated is completely understood by everyone concerned'. For event management, we add the phrase 'and that appropriate action follows'. Understanding the message is vital, as is the two-way nature of all communication. Both these concepts are absolutely essential to the passing of information before and during events.

Before any organisation examines how it communicates, it should consider what are its purposes in communicating. Communication may have several objectives:

- To send a message.
- To have a message received.
- To ensure understanding.
- To achieve correct action.
- To exchange information.

If none of these objectives is met, perhaps the message is not appropriate or effective; communication for events should ultimately produce an action or at the very least a communication exchange. For events it is essential they are all about action, about getting things done; necessary actions are completed to implement the event. There are several methods of communication and the choice is very important.

Verbal communication

Verbal communication is common but it can be unsatisfactory for event management because it is not necessarily witnessed by others or returned by the receiver. It can often be difficult to find time for a face-to-face information exchange, but often it is essential to ease interpersonal relationships and get things done correctly. Verbal communication is essential but don't overuse it.

Non-verbal communication

Always apparent in any face-to-face situation, non-verbal communication consists of body gestures and orientation, facial expression, eye contact and personal appearance. It is a complex interaction, partly unconscious. Everyone that works in an organisation should have a basic knowledge of non-verbal communication, and used appropriately it can help to cement relationships.

Written communication

Written communication is probably the most common in events management and most other contexts, but it is often used excessively and ineffectively. Any paperwork should be kept to the minimum because it is extremely time-consuming to read and write; it can also be demotivating and easily disregarded.

Visual communication

Visual communication is a growing area. Videos are used for product promotion and staff training. An effective logo communicates a message and contributes to the success of an event. Visual communication also helps to create and retain interest among staff.

Electronic communication

The fastest developments are in electronic communication: computers, email, Internet, fax and mobile phones. They bring enormous benefits to event management because events so often take place over large areas, perhaps one big location or several far apart locations. Radios are absolutely essential for most events, so the continuing advances in radio technology are of immense importance.

Figure 3.4 The communication process

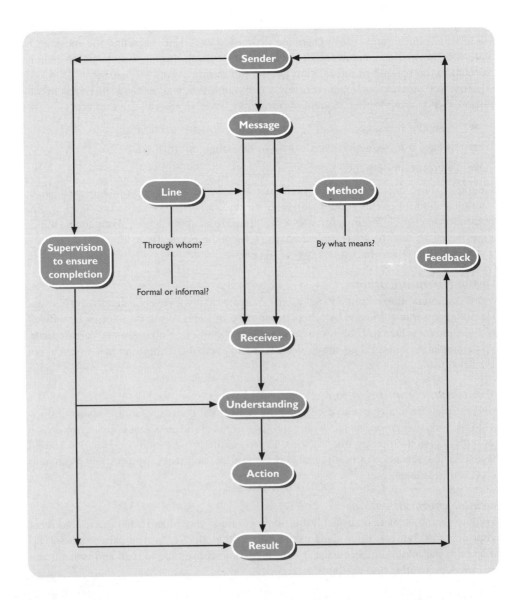

The communication process

Whatever the chosen methods or processes, efficient lines of communication must be established within an organisation, and they must be flexible enough to respond to changes, because changes are almost inevitable (Fig. 3.4). When information is transferred, it should lead to correct understanding and appropriate action. The information should therefore be

- clear
- correct
- concise
- complete
- courteous
- correctly directed

One of the big problems with communication is the ease with which barriers can arise, blocking organisational progress. Communication barriers can appear in various forms: the use of an inappropriate medium; the use of confusing language; the use of ambiguous words and phrases; information overload; interference at different levels; incorrect circulation of information; mistrust between participants; lengthy communication chains and erroneous individual perceptions. All these barriers can cause delays and inactivity, which are fatal for events.

Good communication needs efficient channels and lots of channels, both formal and informal. And good communication is crucial to a successful event. Quite simply, people won't know what to do if they don't get the message! So what does this mean?

- Everyone involved needs to have a clear understanding of the fundamentals:
  - the overall structure of the organisation
  - who has power over, and responsibility for, what
  - what communication methods are to be used
  - how communication is accomplished
  - who has to do what, when and how
- Effective communication systems must be established between all relevant groups and individuals.
- Communication methods (formal and informal) must be simple and clear to all concerned.
- The practical means of communication – email, fax, mobile phones, photocopiers, etc. – should be installed at the appropriate time and made available to all who require them.

Administration

Administration is the formal side of communication. Effective work and communication throughout an event depends upon quality administrative procedures and processes as well as proper administrative staffing and facilities. But this does not mean that systems are set up for their own sake. It is absolutely imperative that we do not become bogged down in unnecessary paperwork and bureaucratic procedures. This is both time-consuming and expensive.

During an event a handwritten note is often adequate; without being typed, it can be faxed or photocopied for internal circulation. High standards of internal presentation are very often unnecessary, wasting your own time and that of your staff. It would be much better to concentrate on items for external circulation, where image may be more important.

Human resources

Without being overly formal or theoretical, it is useful for event organisers to be aware of relevant human factors affecting their operation, e.g. interpersonal relationships, group dynamics, individual needs and other social interaction effects. They should also be aware of personnel concepts such as motivation, involvement and training as well as the more systematic issues such as recruitment and selection.

Interpersonal relationships are a vast and complicated area of study, but even the most basic organiser must recognise how they operate if they are to get the best of their team. If an organisational structure is going to be 'eased' towards its aims, its organisers need to be aware of cliques developing, threatening alliances, personal strengths and weaknesses, individual resentments and egos, and personal conflicts.

Event organisers are not necessarily learned students of the group process; nevertheless, they do implement it. Much event work is done in a group setting; staff will be required to interact as a group from time to time, and the production of a quality event will normally be achieved by using group dynamics. An organiser must consider several aspects of the group and the relationships between its members:

- Do people like and/or *respect* each other and so work well together?
- Does each individual and section have the necessary *status?*
- Is there the *power* to authorise and control the work being undertaken?
- Does each member of the group understand all the *roles* in the group?
- Is the group's *leadership* relevant to its operation?

According to Maslow, an individual's performance is governed by a set of needs:

- psychological
- esteem
- safety
- self-actualisation
- social

We have already mentioned the possible effects on each individual in terms of motivation, but consider how these perhaps unconscious desires will affect the group as a whole. It will not always be feasible to legislate for all these influences, but any leader ignores them at their peril. Especially in events, where a substantial commitment is required, key personnel should be aware of all the social interactions that go on. They are crucially important and must be borne in mind at all times. Events are all about *people* and the relationship between them.

Partnerships

Partnerships form an important aspect of organising events. Be they individuals or groups, public or private, commercial or non-commercial, few agencies can stage an event without entering some sort of partnership that includes other relevant organisations. It is well worthwhile to establish partnerships very early in planning for the event, so that those who will have to be involved, to make it successful, are involved from the start. It is generally true that the earlier the involvement, the greater the commitment.

It is very common for the local enterprise company to be involved in an event along with a sporting or arts body, as well as the local authority and commercial sponsor, all needed for a successful and meaningful event. There can be problems in combining the motives of all these members into an effective partnership, but this relationship will be very beneficial in allowing sufficient finance and resources to maximise the success of the event.

Partnerships are appropriate at all levels of events, and often they are essential. It is worthwhile for any sporting group to enter a fundraising partnership with a local charity; this should prove mutually beneficial, provided there are mutual inputs, e.g. the sports group's organisational skills and the charity's publicity pulling power. It is usually a very good starting point for an event organiser to identify which possible partners may be brought together to make the event happen. These partners may be beneficial because of their special skills; the resources they have available or the funding they can attract to the event. There has to be agreement between all the partners on the purpose of the event and its benefits. Only with these shared aims and objectives, and a clearly defined working relationship, will partnerships work. They are normally essential and many projects have benefited greatly from such partnerships in many different situations.

Within any working committee, organising almost any type of event, it will be beneficial to have other agencies involved; the police and the local authorities are usually well worth having on the committee, if only for information, because it helps to guarantee their support. This again is a type of partnership which evolves because of the need to ensure support from certain agencies; and the best way is to have them actually serving the committee, making the decisions and being part of the whole, instead of as an outside agency advising in a minor way. Large road-running events in the United Kingdom seldom prove a success unless they have a member of the police force on their organising committee.

Self-assessment questions

1. Organisation and communication have been given a separate chapter in this text. What reasons are given for this emphasis and additional attention? Do you feel this is justified? If so, why? If not, why not?

2. Take a small-scale event such as a club tournament or a local art club and suggest
   (a) a suitable organisational structure
   (b) a job remit for two of the key personnel.

3. Information technology has made massive advances in the last five years which greatly benefit event organisers. Identify three particular advances and suggest what difference they have made and how they can best be used to improve event provision.

Chapter Four

Funding

A successful event cannot happen without adequate financial support. The biggest, and perhaps the commonest error, in committing to an event is to do so without securing the necessary funding at a very early stage. To do so will be a concern from start to finish, and may cause the event to be presented in a poor (penny-pinching) manner and quite possibly doom it to failure; indeed, it may have to be aborted at some stage, leaving bad feeling all round.

Two important points:

● It can sometimes be better to abort an event at an early stage, rather than try to persist and eventually present a 'failure', and so acquire a poor image for your organisation.

● Not all events need an enormous amount of money to be successful, especially at a local level.

Remember though, if there are expenses which must be met, it is wise to ensure they can be met right from the start. To check this out, financial viability must be a key issue of any feasibility study, perhaps *the* key issue. In fact, it may be worthwhile to give finance a separate study or to double-check it because it is so important.

Budgeting

Careful budgeting is essential for any event to work well and for it to have credibility. The process of working out the precise details will be one of the true tests of whether the planned event will actually work. It is necessary to budget carefully, both to find out what the event needs in terms of funding and also to provide a monitoring mechanism throughout the event planning and implementation. A variety of problems may be faced in putting a budget together:

● Difficulty in getting enough information on what is required.

● Inexperienced or unskilled managers, who don't focus enough attention on budgeting.

● Inaccurate forecasting of future trends.

● Lack of sufficient detail in available technical requirements.

- Basing budget on false background information.
- Poor reporting or controlling procedures.
- Inability to create the flexibility which is often required in events.

The key step is to carry out proper market research.

The first step in the process of examining funding requirements is to establish what *exactly* the event will cost to stage. A wide range of expenditures will probably need to be anticipated; indeed, later in the book you will find a separate financial check list. Effective estimates can only be made after all the relevant tasks have been identified and costed.

Every item to be achieved must be listed in one column then, placed alongside, should be columns for the likely expenditure and possible income. This will give an exact statement of the forecast figures. It may sound simple, but to obtain accurate figures on all these items can be an onerous task. Nevertheless, it is essential to be as accurate as possible; inaccurate figures can be misleading and may cause severe problems later on. Each activity should be broken down and analysed as follows:

- The precise activity to be carried out.
- The estimated cost of each such activity.
- The benefit from each activity.
- The income (if any) from the activity.
- The necessity of the activity (especially if it is expensive by the standards of the event).
- The place of the activity in the budget priority.
- How the expenditure on the activity can be monitored.
- How the income will come in and how certain it is.

With this process completed, we will be able to consider the costs and benefits of the whole project, before making any final decisions about whether to proceed. There are certain *fixed costs* which will have to be met to stage almost any event, e.g. venue hire, staffing, marketing, insurance. As soon as it is agreed to proceed with the project, most of these costs will have to be incurred, whatever income can be raised to set against them. Other costs will not remain constant; they are *variable costs*. Variable costs will vary according to the size and nature of the event, and perhaps they will have to be adapted during work on the project. Variable costs are exemplified by things like catering, entertainment and accommodation.

It is crucial in budgeting to be as accurate as possible, but it is always advisable to *overestimate expenditure* and to *underestimate income*. To do the opposite is a recipe for disaster. Pessimistic budgeting is a good idea, as long as it doesn't become so pessimistic that people are put off the project.

Special items

VAT

Value added tax (VAT) and its effect on income and expenditure must be taken into account. VAT registration will not be required for many smaller events, though voluntary registration is permitted. The local Customs and Excise office will be happy to advise on the need to register and on the liability of various items to VAT. Care must be taken in recording the ins and outs of items liable to VAT, and its potential effects must be included in the

budget. To forget that all admission fees are liable to VAT would have enormous consequences, reducing anticipated income from this source by 17.5% (at the time of writing).

Inflation

Inflation can have quite profound consequences for budgeting. It can cause estimates to
be out by large amounts; a relatively recent change in the rate of UK inflation produced a
swing of around 10% within a period of 12 to 18 months. Estimates should be calculated
using current prices, but an awareness of the possible impact of inflation must be borne
in mind. Calculations should accompany the estimates to indicate what may happen to
any funding given the likely trends for inflation.

Insurance

Insurance against event failure, cancellation or postponement should be costed and perhaps taken out for a more costly event, even if it is obtainable only at quite a high rate.
Public liability, and even perhaps limited personal accident insurance, must be arranged.
Insurance is another item all too easily forgotten with potentially very expensive consequences. For example, all borrowed equipment must be insured. It is vital to think of everything; items are not automatically covered. And remember to include the cost of insurance
when compiling budgets.

Currency rates

Currency rates can significantly affect the amount of income from some international hap-
penings, particularly events like conferences, where delegate turnout can be affected by
any movements in the exchange rates. A poor turnout of delegates obviously casts doubt
on the viability of these events, as it can produce large variations of income. Delegate income
can change in local currency value from estimating budgets to receiving fees.

Contingencies

The budget should include an amount to cover unforeseen costs. Depending on the size
of the project, allow between 5 and 10% of the total expenditure to cover contingencies.
This can only ever be a guesstimate, but the vital thing is that a realistic figure is set aside
for such emergencies, which will inevitably arise.

Timetable

A financial timetable for events is necessary. This will indicate the precise time when expenditure will occur as well as when the money should come in, where the money will
come from and what it is paying for. Timetabling is an essential part of budgeting when
considering the financial feasibility of any project: calculating interest rates on any bor-
rowings or investments, working out when income is required and later controlling
expenditure against a preset timetable. If a suitable timetable (Fig. 4.1) cannot be worked
out for such expenditure or if compensatory arrangements cannot be made, then it is clear
the event will struggle financially and probably should not proceed. Cash flow is crucial
to any venture.

Financial structures

Soon after it has been agreed that the event is viable and will go ahead, the financial operating structures need to be established quickly. Depending on the level of the event, the

Figure 4.1 A simple time chart for event expenditure

Timetable / Heading	2 years	1 year	6 months	2 months	1 month	event	3 months after	6 months after
Feasibility study	–							
Professional advice	–	–						
Accommodation			20%					
Venue				10%			80%	
Catering				10%	10%	20%	90%	
Advertising				20%	30%		60%	
Insurance			–					
Hire charges							–	
Staff costs	–	–	–	–	–	–	–	–

modus operandi may be very simple, perhaps a treasurer controlling all finances; or it may be very complex, perhaps involving several committees and even paid staff to manage the financial side. Whatever the level, financial structures and systems will be required; control of the lower-level event may require less sophistication, but it requires just as much care.

Where the structure involves committees, there are two main options:

● Finance is a free-standing committee; everyone requests money and awaits their decision.

● Each committee or subcommittee has its own treasurer to look after its allocated budget.

Having committee treasurers may improve efficiency, but there is little doubt that centralised control does deter spending, e.g. the Treasury within the British Cabinet system. Centralised control will be slower, where reports are required to and from the finance committee, but the alternative puts large emphasis on the role of subgroup treasurers. A free-standing finance committee gives greater centralised power, but having committee treasurers gives power to those doing the work.

Which method to choose depends on the nature and scale of the event, the finances and the personalities involved. Everyone needs to be aware of the strengths and weaknesses of both options. However the committee set-up is established, it is important to have a clear structure for financial processing and control (Fig. 4.2). Everyone must know who manages the money, and who authorises and controls expenditure. The various control systems are fundamental to keeping spending within agreed limits at all times. Failure to have meticulous control is a recipe for disaster.

The budget will be established through various stages (Fig. 4.3). This is lengthy but effective, and involves everyone in identifying costs (and possible income). It minimises the chances of mistakes and oversights. The process is vitally important and must be carried out alongside the project aims and objectives, keeping them in focus (Fig. 4.4).

Figure 4.2
Approaches to
financial control.
(a) Each
committee or
subcommittee has
its own treasurer
to look after its
allocated budget.
(b) Finance is a
free-standing
committee

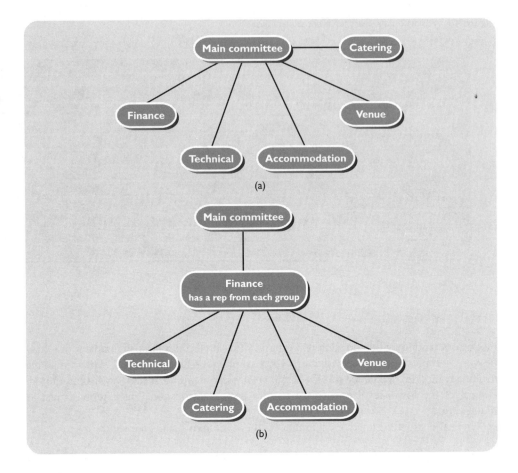

Figure 4.3
How to establish
a budget
democratically

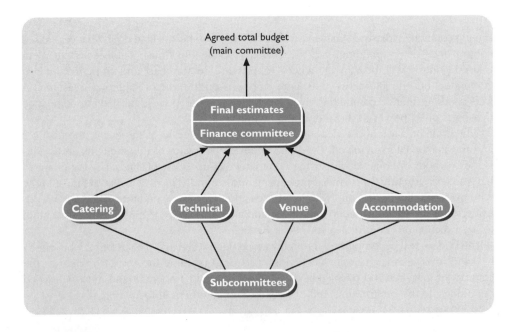

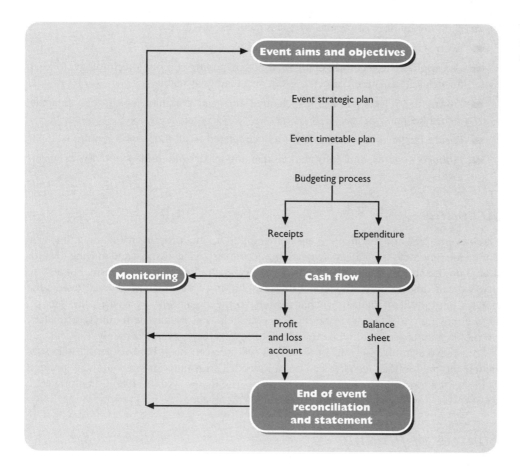

Figure 4.4
Budgeting and
financial control

Control

The careful control of all financial transactions is arguably the most crucial aspect of event management, in the private sector where profit is essential, and in the public and voluntary sectors where large losses can be disastrous. Effective control systems should:

- be understandable
- follow organisational structures
- quickly pick up deviations
- remain flexible
- direct corrective action
- be economical

Events management requires precise and expeditious control that still retains its flexibility. It is vital to have staff (paid or voluntary) that are aware of financial systems and the essence of control. Their role will be central to ensuring continued viability. If this expertise is not freely available within your organisation, then money will be well spent in engaging an accountant or paying for relevant financial advice and support, e.g. an event costings specialist to help with budgets.

Some aspects of an event can be played low-key or fudged; financial control is not one of them. Real expertise and careful attention to detail is imperative. Failure to exercise proper control over budgets will almost certainly lead to chaos. There are several practical steps:

- Limit the number of people who can incur expenditure.
- Keep accurate records of all income and expenditure.
- Use appropriate record-keeping methods, including computer technology, to keep financial information correct, current and readily available.
- Ensure the relevant structures channel financial commitment through financial record keepers.
- Ensure financial information is widely circulated to all those who require it.
- Produce systems and information that are clear and understood by everyone involved.

Accounts

Often events pass and the finances are not wrapped up in a professional manner. It is vital during the process to continue to keep issuing accounts, paying invoices and moving towards a final profit and loss statement. This is necessary as a monitoring mechanism, but also so that we can quickly move towards a final resolution of the finances. For all events the bottom line, profit or deficit, is what matters to the organisers, as well as the sign-off before moving on to the next one. Professional help will usually be required, especially on the final audit – a worthwhile investment for most large events certainly.

To achieve sign-off, the staff of the event will need to push hard to get all bills submitted and paid so that accounts can be produced. This sounds simple, but many projects drag on for a long time trying to tie up finances. The finances of the 1986 Commonwealth games were not finalised until many years after the event.

Sources of funding

So far, we've looked chiefly at expenditure and its control. Vital though it is, do not be too pessimistic about costing or devote too much time to it, otherwise the event may not go ahead at all. It is easy to approach events in a very pessimistic way or to assess them in a negative manner, judging that costs are large and the risks enormous. This is often very true, and without a positive, optimistic and determined approach to fundraising by a key individual or group, many events would not go ahead.

Organisers need to identify possible sources of income and how to secure funding from them. This positive approach – we will find the necessary money – is the only one that will succeed, as long as the focus remains on the aims and objectives. Increasingly many events are undertaken on a purely commercial basis, so a dispassionate analysis must be undertaken; if there is no likelihood of profit, the event will not be staged.

In sport or the arts and with local authority events, other factors, such as publicity, increased tourism and higher status, are considered important enough to justify going ahead despite possible financial loss. If a potentially loss-making event is likely to bring enough of these other benefits, the loss may be underwritten by its organisers.

All organisers will approach bodies for funding and resources; here are some suggestions:

- Local authority leisure department
- Education authority
- Local or national sports council
- Local or national arts council
- Foundation for Sport and the Arts

- Local or national tourist authorities
- National Playing Fields Association
- Uniformed organisations
- Charitable trusts
- Sponsorship agencies
- Professional institutes
- European Union
- National Enterprise Development Agencies
- Business agencies (e.g. Chambers of Commerce)
- Hoteliers
- Local enterprise companies or councils
- Heritage agencies
- Local or national charities
- Voluntary bodies
- Commercial marketing agencies
- Donations
- Fundraising (by group or others)
- Television or radio rights
- The British Council
- The Prince's Trust
- The National Lottery
- Major local employers

In addition, the event itself will be able to produce income from a variety of activities:

- franchising
- donations
- ticketing
- programmes
- entry fees
- fundraising
- raffles
- souvenirs
- catering
- advertising
- licensing (logos, etc.)
- trade exhibitors
- participant contributions
- sales stalls
- bar
- corporate hospitality

Considerable energy has to be expended on income generation; but because it is vital, it is time well spent. It is essential before embarking on an event to ensure that sufficient funding is guaranteed, not just probable. To attract funds, any event or project must have a clearly defined purpose, which is widely accepted as worthwhile. A well-publicised public profile will often be a crucial factor in obtaining financial support from public and private sources.

It may be that support will be in kind rather than straightforward financing. The provision of free (or reduced cost) printing, accommodation, etc., will be of immense assistance and a very worthwhile support package can be drawn up without lots of money changing hands.

Fundraising

Many projects, especially smaller ones, will require some type of fundraising. Fundraising can take many forms, but chosen carefully it can produce quite significant amounts; novel ideas are especially successful. Here are some suggestions:

- sponsored runs, swims, cycles
- dances, discos
- marathon swims, silences, digs
- lotteries, raffles
- car washes
- gambling evenings, e.g. race nights and casino nights.

Sponsorship

Sponsorship is the hardest part of all.

(Robin Knox-Johnson)

Sponsorship is seen by many as the panacea to all funding problems; but we all know there is no such thing as a panacea, and this is certainly true where sponsorship is concerned. Commercial sponsorship can be extremely difficult to find and requires a lot of work to service it. Remember that sponsorship must be seen as a mutually beneficial business arrangement, between sponsor and sponsored, to achieve agreed objectives.

Finding sponsors is never easy and relying on finding them is always dangerous. If it is to be more than a one-off event, there is also a danger of losing sponsors at some time; very few support events or promotions indefinitely. It is always worth remembering they may leave you at any time for any reason, e.g. a government ban on tobacco sponsorship in sport. Be aware of the implications of sponsorship (more later); people have said, perhaps with some justification, that sponsors can be more trouble than they are worth. To obtain a demanding sponsor for a very small amount of money and for a small event could prove to be a waste of time for an event organiser. Significant time must be spent in servicing sponsorship and sometimes this time would be more useful to the event if it were devoted to other forms of support.

Sources of information

- Yellow Pages and local telephone directories.
- Local and national newspapers contain information and adverts.
- Business rates register.
- Business organisations such as Chambers of Commerce and rotary clubs.
- Professionals such as lawyers and architects.
- Participants and their personal contacts.
- High street shops, locally and nationally.
- Libraries: local, regional and national.
- Market research through learned centres, consultancies and other sources.
- Partners that have supported previous events.
- Existing sponsors: companies which already understand the benefits.

What's in sponsorship

It is very important when one is seeking sponsorship to look at the project from the sponsor's viewpoint. After all, if you can't convince yourself that the project is going to be worthwhile, and that a mutually beneficial package can be worked up, it's unlikely that you'll convince a potential sponsor. A sponsorship seeker has to believe in the event to convince anyone else of its worth. To consider the event from a sponsor's viewpoint, ask yourself these questions:

- Does the event match their image?
- How much media exposure will they get?
- How much advertising can they get in and around the event?
- Can the company name be incorporated in the title of the event?
- Will there be a possibility of corporate hospitality?
- Will the sponsor meet famous people?
- Are there other promotional opportunities?
- Will the name be synonymous with the event? (e.g. Cornhill Insurance and test match cricket)
- Does the event match up to their target audience?
- Is it value for money?

If you assess there will be significant return for a sponsor, then proceed to look for some commercial benefit. If you can deliver this, then chase the sponsors hard.

Some tips on looking for sponsorship

Use imagination and innovation
A bright, new idea is much more likely to persuade someone to spend their money, than a hackneyed, old project which has been staged often by many people in the past. An approach to a new company is also worthwhile, as the novelty may interest them.

Put in the marketing effort
Ensure the product and price are correct and everyone knows about the quality of the event. If the project is widely known, there is much more chance of attracting interest from potential sponsors. It is important to promote the organisation's and/or the agency's image and good practice.

Clearly define the type of market
Sponsors like to know the types of market that may be created. If the participants are affluent middle-aged people, then credit card companies might be quite keen to work with the event organisers.

Consider changing the nature of your activity, event or promotion
Adapt the event to suit a sponsor's idea rather than just repeat your old unsuccessful methods, or persist with something which may not specifically suit their desires. The project and the organisers should be flexible enough to adapt to a reasonable sponsor's requirements.

Try to access your sponsors through local business groups

Approach sponsors through the Town women's Guild, the Chamber of Commerce or the Rotary Club, as well as through the media and in person. These groups can provide ideas as well as contacts.

Assess respective images

Check that any images are compatible and try to work with groups where there is an obvious tie-up or correspondence. Sponsors need to be compatible with the event and its participants.

Approach unlikely targets

There may be somebody who has never been approached before and who would like to sponsor an event. Perhaps yours can provide the ideal opportunity. Until recently nobody had ever thought of legal practices advertising and sponsoring events, but now it has become quite common.

Do the necessary research

Examine the markets in which companies seem to be operating and assess whether their target age group is the same as yours. Doing detailed research using newspapers and other media, and in the local library, will pay dividends in the long run. You will come over as a knowledgeable sponsorship seeker and make a good impact on potential sponsors.

Check existing sponsors

Find out what active companies are already sponsoring; this will indicate the fields that interest them. Banks often look for young secondary school pupils on the verge of opening their first account, potential customers reputedly for life. But this does not mean that companies will ignore other areas; if they already sponsor one sort of event, they may still be interested in a different sort.

Try to start with media support

If two or three papers, local or national, or perhaps a radio station will work with organisers and give some constructive plugs at an early stage, then sponsorship may be more easily attracted. The support of the media will be crucial to both the organiser and the sponsor throughout the project, getting their support and enthusiasm early on will be very advantageous.

Who to approach

Choosing who to approach can often be the most difficult, but perhaps the most crucial decision. Often one can totally misdirect the approach and so fail to find a sponsor for what is a very worthwhile competition, exhibition or conference. There is very little point in a mailshot to sponsors. One has got to do a great deal of careful thinking and research into who may be interested in sponsoring a project and why it would be appropriate for their company. Meticulous market research is vital; know the potential companies, their policies and the key individuals to approach.

It is common knowledge that a number of companies are interested in sponsorship targeted at specific community groups. For example, it is likely that high street banks will be happy to sponsor events for young people (aged 15 to 21) since they will be keen to have their name associated with this age group; they are potentially lifelong customers, a very valuable commodity.

Many finance houses sponsor the arts, believing that it gives them a positive identity with influential business people. Local companies tend to support local events. Consumers in different income groups will support different events, and the events will therefore attract different sponsors. Companies have target markets. It is likely that soft drink companies will be keen to be associated with marathons or major sporting manifestations, e.g. the constant Coca-Cola and Pepsi battle to be involved in the world's major sporting events.

The key is to approach a relevant company with your proposition. It is unlikely that a company with a fast-car, modern and upmarket image will sponsor a seminar on issues affecting elderly people. The problem is to keep very aware of companies and their current target markets. Both of them can change; nowadays some retired people have considerable spending power.

Sponsorship of almost anything can be a very cost-effective public relations exercise, often much cheaper than many other forms of marketing, especially advertising. This is a useful argument to employ on potential sponsors.

What to offer

Assuming that one has contacted a likely company, the next step is to prepare an attractive, realistic and deliverable package of benefits. In return for their support, the sponsoring agency must be assured of some payback. It is also beneficial to approach sponsors at the concept stage, giving them an opportunity to make suggestions instead of presenting something cut and dried. Sponsors like their say in the detail of what is delivered, so early consultation is helpful. The detail and the presentation of this pack are crucial, and only if it matches up to the expectations of the audience will you have any chance of success. It is equally essential that the package is well thought out and is genuinely achievable. If an offer is an overtly unrealistic package, the sponsor will notice and will be frightened off right away. Any proposal should be as bright and eye-catching as possible; here are some items to include:

- market research
- background of the event and the organisers
- level of involvement requested
- benefits on offer
- marketing opportunities

How to put the proposal

An appointment should ideally be arranged with the key person in the organisation of the potential sponsor. This should be arranged by telephone, followed up by written confirmation and delivery of the sponsorship package several days before the meeting, giving them an opportunity to study the document. Sometimes a meeting may be impossible, so the project director may be totally reliant on a letter or the package eliciting an answer from the potential sponsor. It is still advisable to set deadlines and say that they will be contacted by phone on a set date to assess their reaction to the package, to discuss details and to consider possible changes to make the proposal more suitable. It is vital to keep your promises about letters, meetings and phone calls; otherwise the proposal will end up in the bin. Getting to the stage of a meeting means there is a 70% chance of finalising a deal, as long as their is a sound case and it is presented with commitment and enthusiasm.

Making the play

- entertain
- give history
- create image
- put on a show
- make presentation
- use event features, personalities, photos and audiovisuals

Agreement or contract

It is essential that a sponsorship agreement, short or long, is laid out in writing and signed by both parties, detailing exactly what is to be given in sponsorship and exactly what is expected in return. It may also be necessary to include penalties if either party fails to reach the specified levels indicated in the contract or agreement. This may seem a little draconian, but it is based on experience and is certainly the best way to proceed; it solves any problem, either from the sponsor trying to withdraw at the last minute or looking later for benefits which were never previously requested. Such disputes can lead to dissatisfaction. It is always sensible to have an agreement to refer back to, in order to clarify any possible sources of disagreement before or during the event.

Do everything you can

If you are lucky enough to get a sponsor, especially a good, firm but fair one, then work hard to keep them. Perhaps this is the area in which most organisers, particularly voluntary ones, fall down. They fail to recognise the commercial agreement they have entered into and the importance of carrying out their side of it and, if possible, bettering it. They feel they can take the money and not produce the goods. This is not the case, and a sponsor will always expect the details of the promised package to materialise. If there is any doubt about what is to be done, it should be resolved in the sponsor's favour.

It is a good idea to sign a sponsor on a two-year or three-year agreement; often they will want at least a trial year to see whether they will commit themselves further. It is well worthwhile to keep that sponsor happy (assuming you are happy with them) because this will save a massive amount of work in seeking a new sponsor for your next event. Remember, always deliver what you said you would deliver.

In-kind support

For some local events, the biggest in-kind supplier may become the principal sponsor and there may in fact be no transfer of money, but a supply of goods or services which are a large cost of the event. It is common for the local authority to be a major sponsor, helping through providing facilities, catering or organisational assistance free of charge. Equally, drink companies, communication companies, transport companies, computer companies and confectionery suppliers can often become major sponsors without any money actually changing hands.

It is a very good idea to identify all the requirements for a project, and then draw up a corresponding list of possible suppliers to approach for in-kind support. Approach everyone and try to convince them of the benefits of supporting the event. Never leave any stone unturned or any potential source untapped. For many events, this type of sponsorship is all that is required, and in most cases it is undoubtedly easier to obtain than cash.

As an event organiser, normally running on a very limited budget, one has got to adopt the slogan, 'never pay for anything you can get for nothing'. In truth you get nothing for nothing, but at least you can get something from a sponsor instead of paying for it in cash.

Making sponsorship work

As an event organiser it will often be hard to make the sponsorship deal work as effectively as it could. Everyone must make every effort to do so, but it is often useful to delegate people just to ease the relationship and become the internal PR or sponsor liaison person.

It is also very important to emphasise to the sponsor from the beginning that for their organisation to get the very best out of the sponsorship, they should be looking to invest in others ways into the deal. It is often said that a sponsor putting £5000 into an event should set aside another £5000 to maximise their PR benefit from the event. For example, they could benefit from related advertising, corporate hospitality, logo identity, promotional items like T-shirts, and additional decorating touches for the event venue to highlight their involvement. All these additional inputs will maximise the sponsorship benefits for the company involved. A little innovative thinking in this area can be enormously helpful.

Practical sponsorship

Some practical issues can help the whole process and ensure a good corporate image for both parties, leading to a successful sponsorship deal. Not all of them apply on every occasion, but here are some ideas that are worth considering:

- An accurate budget breakdown is given to potential sponsors, so they are aware of what their contribution means.
- Potential sponsors are invited to hospitality at current events, thereby selling future events.
- The sponsorship price is not pitched too high or too low.
- The correct organisations, people and agencies are targeted; image and resources must be appropriate.
- The chances of success are maximised by using all the available market information.
- All contacts, including social contacts, are followed for a lead to possible sponsors.
- A professional approach is taken at all times.
- The price is right and the package is well prepared.
- The initial approach may be in writing, but it must be followed up quickly with personal contact.
- Sponsors must be kept informed at all times, even about failures.
- Honesty at all times is crucial to developing a partnership.
- Care for your sponsors; attend to all their (reasonable) requirements as soon as they are identified.
- Good advance planning will help fit into potential sponsors budgeting plans.
- Hard work will maximise your sponsor's return.
- Be creative, flexible and innovative in sponsorship delivery ideas.
- Be aware of developments in the business world and possible 'opponents' in seeking sponsorship.
- Joint debriefing and appraisal sessions are essential.

To attract sponsorship the event must be right. A poor event will be potentially disastrous for everyone involved. The organiser's technical skills and knowledge must be used to get the event right in planning and delivery, so making the sponsor's support justified.

In summary, sponsorship with all the allied hard work can be very worthwhile. Both parties must work to make it effective and at no time must the event organisers promise what they cannot deliver. On the other hand, there is a tendency among event organisers to undersell their product, especially when they are seeking support from sponsors or agencies like tourist authorities or enterprise councils. Remember that events can be a phenomenal boost to an area. The returns can be enormous to the local economy. The Edinburgh Festival, the Isle of Wight Yacht Races or the many garden festivals are all examples of events which have, or had, a profound effect on the local area in terms of morale, financial return, tourist and commercial return.

Don't be afraid to quote successful examples, but avoid any grandiose or unrealistic claims for your event. If you have something to sell, sell it hard then deliver the goods. Martin Morton has suggested this sequence:

1. Prepare the approach.   5. Present the package.
2. Explore the opportunities.   6. Never give up.
3. Select the businesses.   7. Follow it up.
4. Time the approach.   8. Audit the organisation.

It is also essential to conclude the sponsorship arrangement with a comprehensive report on the event detailing the successes of the deal. Prepared for the sponsor and the event management team, it should contain the following items:

Marketing success Based on meaningful research during and after the event, it will be necessary to state what impact the project has had on the image of the sponsor and what it has done for them in other ways, e.g. commercial benefit, corporate hospitality and market penetration. This needs to be based on concrete facts and figures, not some perceived or imaginary benefits.

Press coverage Copies of all appropriate cuttings, photographs or even audiotapes from radio, should be part of the report giving a clear indication of the level of publicity the sponsor gained.

Promotional materials Copies of all posters, tickets, brochures or other promotional items should be part of the report, to indicate the image and exposure the sponsor gained.

Event analysis Comprehensive and clear facts and figures, as well as stated opinions of key individuals, should be presented in any final report, to give the sponsor an accurate indication of information, such as attendance figures and performance levels.

Gratitude A clear statement of thanks should explain all the sponsor has done and the crucial nature of their support. It is best when it comes from participants and spectators as well as organisers.

The future Proposals for future relationships should accompany the conclusion and thanks. Obviously, everybody hopes the sponsorship will continue.

Giving such professional feedback will be a key factor in retaining a sponsor, or even attracting a new one. Any sponsor will be interested to see how past events have been achieved and reported.

Potential blocks to successful sponsorship

Many things can upset a sponsor relationship, but it is important that the organisers don't cause them and that they look at all the issues carefully to ensure there are no unnecessary blocks on their part. Here are a few items which can cause problems if not handled properly:

No clearly stated goals If there is a lack of clarity and purpose for the event, it will be harder to attract sponsors.

Lack of strategic approach If there is no clearly thought-out strategy for attracting sponsors, any work will be ad hoc and probably less successful.

Are the needs satisfied? In providing a service, it is important to look at satisfying somebody's needs, and if we want sponsorship, we have to look at satisfying the sponsor's needs. If they are not going to be satisfied, they are not likely to support us in the venture.

Publicity Throughout the project, publicity needs to be interesting and the right measures need to be taken to obtain it; publicity is the lifeblood of sponsorship.

Reputation The combined reputation of the sponsor and organiser must be credible and support a worthwhile project. If either has a reputation that somehow endangers the project, then perhaps no partnership should be entered into.

Targeting Necessary steps must be taken to ensure the event audience is clearly identified and potential sponsors are properly targeted. Potential sponsors will expect to receive a clear proposal.

Effort There needs to be a significant effort put in to gain sponsorship and thereafter to service it. If staff are not willing to put in the time and effort, the search for sponsorship is futile.

Staff time It is going to take a significant amount of time to find sponsorship and ultimately service it. This needs to be worthwhile and efficient. If not, perhaps other ways of raising the money can be found, methods requiring lower long-term effort.

Expertise The organisation must have enough expertise to find the sponsorship, deliver the goods and service the sponsorship throughout the project; and indeed the expertise to lay down the proposals for sponsors in advance. A shortage of expertise will be damaging if not fatal, although expertise can sometimes be bought in.

Despite this apparently negative final list, there is a significant and growing amount of money available for the right events, properly presented.

Self-assessment questions

1. You are to act as fundraiser for the local Christmas pantomine, which will feature largely young people of school age. Suggest who you might approach for financial support and why.

2. For the pantomine mentioned in Question 1, prepare a budget estimate, giving the anticipated income and expenditure. Also give a two-paragraph report which you would present to the committee on the most important items in the budget. Suggest the structure and mechanisms you would like to see for financial control.

3. Naturally sponsors will be required for this pantomine. Identify possible companies, individuals or agencies to target; suggest what benefits could be offered and how the presentation would be made to each of them.

Chapter Five

Marketing

Marketing is perhaps one of the most overused and least understood terms in many management situations, including event management. The most important concern is that everyone involved needs to be quite clear that marketing is an *approach* not just a *concept*. It must be a method of operation pervading the whole organisation, not just a token statement of intent or a stated concern over promotion. The whole project management process must be dominated by the desire to market the event to all necessary parties, not just spectators and participants, but sponsors, media, VIPs, staff, advertisers and the public.

There are many definitions of marketing:

> *Marketing is an integrated process of producing, distributing and selling goods and services. (Source unknown)*

> *Marketing is the integrated effort necessary to discover, create and arouse and satisfy customer needs – at a profit. (Source unknown)*

> *Marketing is a management process responsible for identifying, anticipating and satisfying customer requirements – profitability. (The Institute of Marketing)*

> *Marketing is so basic that it cannot be considered a separate function. . . . It is the whole business seen from the point of view of its final result, that is, from the customer's point of view. (Peter Drucker)*

But Lyndsey Taylor's acronym sums up the key characteristics and messages that genuine marketing should contain:

Meeting customer needs
Attracting new customers
Reacting to market trends
Keeping up with competitors
Encouraging customer loyalty
Targeting specific customers
Identifying market opportunities
Noting customer feedback
Getting it right every time

There are few definitions of marketing for events; however, any that emphasise the process and the people will be appropriate. My own preference is for something like Phillip Kotler's:

> *The marketing concept holds that the key to achieving organisational goals consists of determining the needs and wants of target markets (defined as the set of actual and potential buyers of product) and delivering the desired satisfactions more effectively and efficiently than competitors.*

Or Michael Hall's:

> *The function of event management that can keep in touch the event's participants and visitors (consumers), read their needs and motivations, develop products that meet these needs, and build a communication programme which expresses the event's purpose and objectives.*

The fundamental principle is that the customer is all-important. Everything from conception to conclusion must be performed with customers (all of them) in mind. Marketing has traditionally been applied to products, but it has recently become a recognised tool of the service industries. In events management we do produce a product, but the important factor is how it is produced, the process; and even the end product is less about tangible objects than about feelings and experiences.

Events are like services; they are distinctly different from industrial product's. Here are some of their special features:

Intangibility Customers feel the benefits and the enjoyment, but they can't touch the event.

Perishability The fun is transitory; it is rare to have lasting evidence of the event.

Inseparability Customers associate one event with the next; they identify with the organising agency's reputation for quality.

Consistency Customers demand consistency and it is important to achieve it.

Lack of ownership Events don't belong to anyone but they are temporarily enjoyed by many.

Event customers are going to be very keen on how they are treated, and what facilities and services are laid on; they are not content to see an art exhibition or a sporting contest in the most basic of conditions. Over recent years many providers of large spectacles have had to radically improve the level and quality of facilities and services available to patrons. Ageing theatres and football grounds are no longer adequate for their clients, who now have much more sophisticated expectations. This element, customer care, is what singles out the service sector from manufacturing industries. And it is vital to events. True quality in this area must be the constant target for all event organisers.

Customer care

Customer care is a buzz phrase across all businesses now, particularly service industries like the hospitality trade. It is a major and vital part of event management. Careful consideration needs to be given to all event customers. If they enjoy the event, they will come back themselves and maybe invite their friends to the next part of the programme or a future event planned by the same agency.

Customer care must begin as soon as the customer reaches the event, or starts on the road to the event. The directions, the car park, the reception areas, the premises and all the facilities involved must be of the highest possible standard and ready for the customer's arrival and use. Customer care is best achieved by putting yourself in the customer's shoes and observing the event from their point of view. What is it that you want or that you need? If you need something, so will the customer.

Customer care must be seen as something that concerns everyone involved in the organising body, from top manager to car park attendant. Without customers, the whole event will be futile, so everyone must believe in serving the customer. Some members of the organising group may be serving the players in a football tournament; other members may be serving the spectators, the referees, the VIPs or the sponsors.

Each section will have its own specific customers, but it is just as important for all groups to create a positive image and impression with each other's customers. They must try to do everything possible for their specific customers and ultimately for everyone who attends the event. The attitude must be: Let's do all we can to avoid anything upsetting our customers or spoiling their enjoyment of the event; we are all in the business of maximising their pleasure. We must try to give our customers more than they expected.

Customer care involves the very basics of looking clean, tidy and presentable; wearing the uniform or badge of the event; making quite clear who you are and what you are there to do; and learning a few basic phrases in foreign languages to make your customer feel more welcome at the event. Some visitors may be making their first trip to your country or region. Remember that the customer is king. Be reverent to the king.

Although events are about people and service, their marketing does have many similarities with other commercial situations.

Factors in marketing

Marketing can be affected by a number of issues, some controllable, some not, but organisers must be aware of them:

Location Consider the attractiveness and accessibility of the location as well as environmental factors such as traffic and scenery.

Social factors The attitude of friends and colleagues will affect people's attitudes to what is appropriate.

Cultural influences Different groups in society, e.g. ethnic origin, social class, part of the country, will see different events in different ways.

Fashion During certain periods in history, certain types of project will be in vogue and will attract large attendances.

Political factors Local and central government will pursue areas for support that fit with their beliefs.

Economic factors Assess how much money is available at a corporate level and an individual level; consider exchange rates and similar economic factors.

Philosophy The beliefs and attitudes of groups, individuals and other agencies will affect the range of events provided.

A marketing checklist

1. Know your organisation thoroughly and be able to identify potential market segments and target groups.

2. Know your event goals; draw up a budget and a strategic plan to achieve them.

3. Know you consumer; talk to relevant groups, visit related establishments and learn from the ideas of others.

4. Know your competitors; find out what they have to offer, their facilities and their programmes.

5. Keep in touch with others in the same business; use public relations and hospitality to make friends with the press.

6. Identify possible gaps in the market for your event; test for preliminary ideas and think through the process very carefully.

7. Look at ways to increase the size and status of the event, and make the most of any merchandising opportunities.

8. Measure the profits made in the event.

9. Create your own image for the event; begin with an efficient reception, avoid queues, and employ smart and appropriate staff at all levels.

10. Be innovative, accept original concepts and risk; be flexible to accentuate all possibilities.

11. To get publicity be original; firsts are important and always remembered.

12. Changing circumstances always mean new opportunities for promotion and publicity; take every opportunity that occurs.

13. Motivate people; make the staff part of a team that is willing to identify with the event and publicise it.

14. Make sure that every aspect of the event is designed specifically for the people who will come to it; be customer orientated.

15. Remember that 'freebies' are important, everybody likes something for nothing; a sticker or badge will help people to remember the event, before, during and after; it will also remind them of last time's positive experiences and it could persuade them to attend the next one.

16. Make the rules of the event fair and appropriate for everyone.

17. Make the facilities attractive and clean; create a quality image.

18. Make the facilities accessible with appropriate maps, signposting, parking, etc.

19. Work hard to let everyone, internal and external, know exactly what's happening at all times; lack of information is the worst type of publicity.

20. 'Sell' the event to everyone: staff, financiers, sponsors and customers.

Consider most or all of these aspects for each event. A great deal of effort will have to be expended on a true marketing approach. Support and enthusiasm for marketing your project will not simply appear, it needs to be cultivated. Marketing concepts are widely applicable commercially and are also relevant to events. Market research, self-analysis, targeting and marketing mix are all useful to help get the ideas just right.

Market research

Market research is concerned with measurement and analysis of markets. A suitable definition is as follows:

The objective gathering, recording, and analysing of all facts relating to the provision of services for the appropriate consumer.

Extensive research before an event can help to answer some questions:

- Is it serving a useful purpose?
- Will people be interested in it?
- Will people attend and/or participate?
- Will it be financially viable?
- Will it be favourably received by the business community?
- Will it be favourably received by the media?
- Will it be appropriate to the targeted group?

This general information, perhaps coupled with more specific details, will help to decide whether the event is relevant, interesting and viable. There is little point in proceeding with a project if the research results are negative. Good research is vital and must not be ignored, once obtained. No event should proceed without some market research; the complexity of the event will determine how much and what kind. The cost of market research needs to be examined, and existing information should be checked to see what is already available.

Market research can help to reduce uncertainty and therefore the risk of failure; it can also help to plan an effective marketing strategy and to analyse how successful it may be. Effective research should follow these guidelines:

- The objectives must be very clear.
- There must be a cost-effective plan of how best to ascertain the relevant information.
- State how the plan will be implemented.
- Explain what plans are necessary for reviewing the process and the information.

It may be that a major public research programme will be necessary for large events, but for smaller projects this is often too expensive and too complex. There are lots of sources of relevant secondary information:

- personal records
- staff knowledge
- public libraries
- government departments
- universities and colleges
- trade unions and professional associations
- marketing research agencies
- others agencies

Other agencies include the Arts Council, the Sports Council, tourist authorities or National Heritage.

Direct research can be carried out by self-completion, postal questionnaires, telephone interviews, personal interviews or group discussion. The questions must be carefully designed to avoid error and inaccuracy; and any interviewers must be reliable and unbiased, so the results will be meaningful. The results must be painstakingly reviewed after analysis. Computers will be key to the collation of results, but the interpretation must be undertaken cautiously, with an expert eye, examining all the possible meanings of the data collected. Try to get at what is actually correct, not what you hope to be true. Only genuine conclusions will be meaningful and constructive in developing an event.

SWOT *analysis*

Fundamental to any marketing project is a situational analysis – past, present and future – and how the venture will fit into it. Situational analysis is best undertaken by SWOT:

Strengths
the internal strengths of the organisation

Weaknesses
the internal weaknesses of the organisation

Opportunities
the external opportunities which may arise

Threats
the external threats facing the organisation

The results of this work will obviously vary considerably, depending on the exact nature and demands of the specific event. Here are a few possibilities that may apply to a wide range of events.

Strengths

- staff ability
- detailed specialist knowledge
- local reputation
- political support
- enthusiasm and commitment

Weaknesses

- poor transport framework
- limited financial resources
- lack of general management skills
- poor public image

Opportunities

- increased public awareness
- developing partnerships
- financial returns
- changing attitudes
- offering new possibilities

Threats

- lack of commercial support
- competition from similar promotions
- changes in funded priorities
- economic trends

SWOT analysis helps with realistic planning for the whole enterprise, but especially with the marketing strategy (more on this shortly).

Target groups

To make any marketing work, it must be quite clear at whom it is aimed. For many promotions the audience may be quite varied: old and young, fit and unfit, academic and artisan. But some events will target a more specific group: a venture may be aimed specifically at women or the 50+ age group or Gaelic speakers or the local business community or the European market. This will be one of the questions answered by good market research. Whatever the group, it must be clearly identified and targeted.

For events, the targets may be different for different aspects (Fig. 5.1). It may be necessary to identify targets – potential participants, potential spectators, potential sponsors and potential staff – all from different areas and requiring differing marketing to obtain their support. Market research and careful use of previous knowledge will identify the groups relevant to particular events. The next step is to ascertain each group's needs and devise a plan

Figure 5.1
Some target
groups for event
marketing

to meet them. This will greatly assist with overall event planning, but especially the marketing strategy; indeed, more than one strategy may be used to target the identified groups.

Marketing mix

Marketing is often portrayed as a complex concept with a great deal of mystique, perhaps for the greater glory of the marketing companies or personnel. In essence it is a simple combination of factors to get the right balance for any commercial activity. There are four primary factors:

- place
- price
- product
- promotion

The correct balance for an enterprise is called the marketing mix. The consideration given to each factor will vary from one event to another, but on each occasion all four factors need to be balanced. Balance cannot be achieved by ignoring one of them. For events, the following definitions apply:

Place This has several aspects:

- venue
- accommodation
- ancillary facilities
- signposting
- maps
- car parking
- catering location
- transport
- emergency access
- host town
- region
- county
- environmental conditions
- geographic location, etc.

Product This is the end result – the event, the tournament, exhibition, seminar or show. It also involves all the ancillary contributions like programmes, presentation, quality production and customer care.

Price Can the event be provided at a price acceptable to customers? Can price packages be put together to support group attendance or tourist rates?

Promotion This has several aspects:

- advertising
- media relations
- publicity
- merchandising
- pamphlets
- posters
- logo
- displays

Figure 5.2 Marketing mixes. Local authorities are not primarily concerned about the price of the product and they may have a limited promotional budget; the product and the venue will need to be very good. Profit is paramount to commercial organisations; the price of the event will determine the number of exhibitors; place will be less important than promotion, especially image and awareness; the exhibitors will supply the products

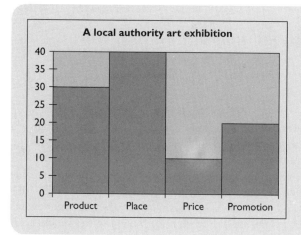
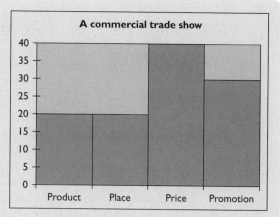

The good event manager will balance these aspects to produce a good marketing mix. The adjustment of this balance from concept to completion will fundamentally affect the outcome of the project (Fig. 5.2).

The foremost thoughts must be for people and their quality care; however, the whole operation at every stage and at all levels, must acknowledge the elements of the marketing mix.

For some services, and certainly for events, there are a number of other P's which should be included:

People People are the crucial factor in delivering a good event, especially proper customer care and effective teamwork. Well-trained and capable, people are a major marketing tool.

Packaging Packaging concerns the way events are presented, whether as part of a season or festival, in a tournament or as a one-off. Any marketing will depend on the package, e.g. a family package or a season ticket.

Partnership The support of others and their marketing presence can be a significant benefit.

Programming When an event is scheduled will be a major tool in its marketing. It should suit the arts or canvassing calendar and it should create interest by using other projects around it.

Through balancing all the P's, a skilled manager can devise a strategy to maximise the success of a particular event.

Promotion

Many aspects should be considered under promotion: image, logo, advertising, media, public relations, selling, souvenirs, presentation, merchandising and publicity. It is a common misconception to treat promotion as a synonym for marketing; it is not. Promotion is the communicating part of marketing – how the product can be brought to the attention of the public and prospective participants. It also deals with the image and presentation of the product; in our case the event. By addressing consumers with a purpose-designed promotional scheme, the aim is to achieve AIDA:

Attention
Interest
Desire
Action

Logo

An appropriate logo can be a crucial part of any public image. It is important to give it careful thought and to consult relevant agencies and authorities before finalising the design. Its impact on merchandising and souvenirs can have a sizeable effect on income.

It used to be common to look for relatively simple logos using a single colour, but now multicoloured and often multi-image logos are used for international manifestations. This is to maximise colour combinations and possibilities, so maximising sales. For larger events this can be a gold mine, but smaller events should be wary of buying in too much stock of items they may not sell.

A good logo should

- reflect the event
- pass on what it is about
- be attractive and eye-catching
- portray an event image
- give relevant messages
- be colourful (preferably)

Mascot

Also related to image, any event of any size should have its own mascot, as long as it can afford one. A mascot can help to promote the event in various ways, especially with certain target groups. The mascot must be closely identified with the event; it should be appropriate, relevant and attractive; it should portray the project image and it should be saleable.

Advertising

Well-targeted, cost-effective advertising can make the difference between success and failure. But most advertising is expensive, so it has to be done with specific objectives in mind and at a level which suits the event. It is often possible to get editorial coverage as an alternative to newspaper advertising, and pick up other space by way of low-key sponsorship from bus companies or billboard firms.

But despite its cost, successful advertising is invaluable, and the most appropriate sites should be chosen from a list of possible locations. Yet again, simple questions are among the most important:

- Why?
- Who for?
- What exactly?
- Which media?
- Where?
- When?
- How much?
- Who judges the response?
- How is it evaluated?

A successful advertising campaign has several key features:

- Promote awareness of the event.
- Pass on knowledge of relevant event details.
- Encourage the desire to participate in or attend the event.
- Promote the conviction that the event is worthwhile.
- Aim to establish attendance patterns in the long run for future events.
- Encourage the decision that turns the interest into attendance or participation.
- Promote the event image and logo.
- Be positive and interesting to attract attention.

Local press and radio advertising are not cheap but may well be cost-effective, especially for young people and commercial radio. Television advertising is expensive but can be very effective in reaching mass audiences. Cost is obviously a determining factor but the chosen medium should also reflect the target audience. Certain newspapers are read by certain groups and local commercial radio is said to have close contact with a younger audience, i.e. under 30. Targeted advertising is necessary and should prove effective.

Media relations and publicity

Media relations and publicity should be given a lot of attention. A well-planned publicity campaign should run alongside any advertising campaign. Ideally this drive should be spread over a period of months, building up to a peak shortly before the event. Early warning allows potential participants and spectators to book the event into their diaries and prevents potential clashes with rival attractions. Some publicity will have to be paid for, but there are ways of obtaining a good deal for little or no cost. The secret is imagination and attention to detail. The Internet is one way to obtain a significant amount of publicity relatively cheaply and easily.

Early contact with the media is essential. Think about a catch phrase, as well as a logo, to identify your event. Try to get a public figure involved or to open the event. This should help to get local publicity. Other media outlets that can be contacted are national and regional newspapers, trade and professional magazines, radio, television and teletext. There are also opportunities through direct mail, hoardings, national agency events lists, car stickers and word of mouth. Don't be shy about contacting the media. They rely on people telling them what's happening, especially when there's not much sport or political news. Some general points to remember when dealing with the media:

- The media need you as much as you need them.
- You know more about the technicalities of your subject than they do.
- Be confident during an interview; the cooler you appear, the easier the hot seat becomes.
- With a bit of imagination, it is quite possible to get thousands of pounds worth of free publicity.

Some guidelines on getting media attention

A *catchy headline* on a press release will attract attention and create good images in the editor's mind. The famous newspaper headline 'Freddie Starr ate my Hamster' caused major nationwide interest although it was inaccurate. A press release must have an interesting angle, and it must place it very near the start. All press releases should be targeted for local or national consumption.

Always be *positive* about the event. Do not allow news to be twisted so it becomes negative. Journalists may be more interested in bad news than good, and may try to adjust what is happening. Be prepared for this and resist it as much as possible; seize any opportunity to convey positive information.

With the correct *emphasis*, a local story can quickly become national. Perhaps it is a national first or something totally unique; a recent non-story on the recycling of wellies due to their high plastic content made national news on British radio.

A number of publications give *addresses and telephone numbers* for the editors of relevant newspapers, magazines, television and radio stations, etc. It is very important to get the name of an individual if you want them to respond. A general letter to the editor or subeditor is not going to be as successful as a letter to a specific reporter, particularly one who specialises in your subject area.

A. & C. Black publish the *Writers and Artist's Year Book*, an annual list of useful names and addresses. Organisations like the Sports Council and Arts Council may also be able to give a detailed list of specialists who may be worth contacting about a particular event.

Think long and hard about *who* may be interested in what you are doing. Do not be afraid to *approach* people.

Email or fax are now often the preferred method, but conversation on the telephone can often arouse interest which no press release, no matter how well written, can achieve. A day's *phoning* will often set up more publicity for your event, and much more quickly, than two or three days' writing and sending press releases.

Spending *time with a journalist* or editor can be well worthwhile in setting up coverage of the event, a good working lunch can be a sound investment.

Press releases

Many 'no news' press releases land on editors' desks every day. If you want your event to be noticed, the press release must be interesting. Do not expect the twenty-third Inter-Regional Basketball Tournament to catch the eye of a journalist. It is essential to turn this routine event into some sort of story, preferably a first, e.g. the first time the British champions have visited Newcastle, or the first time the top three British basketball players have taken part in this tournament.

It is essential that the press release starts with the news in the first two lines, very often all that is read. The press release should be brief; use no more that two sheets of A4, and one is enough to get some interest. Be succinct, clear and interesting. Use double spacing within paragraphs and four lines between paragraphs. Make sure the margins are wide.

Provide the contact name and telephone number at the end of the press release and address it to an individual at a specific publication or radio station. A sample press release is shown on p. 144.

Golden rules of media liaison

1. When dealing with the media it is always better to be proactive rather than reactive.
2. Always find a named contact, writing 'to whom it may concern' usually ends up in the bin.
3. Try to think in headlines, especially when writing a press release. This may catch the eye.
4. When talking to journalists, it is safest to assume that nothing is off the record.

5. Find the best spokesperson for the event or promotion and appoint them as the media contact. This ensures a consistent line is issued from the organisation. Having different people speak to the press is a recipe for disaster.

6. Retain copies of all radio, television or other media coverage. This is important for the event and will help to keep sponsors happy. It may also help individual media contacts to hone their performance. Press cuttings agencies tend to be expensive, so they may not be financially viable except for major events.

Press conferences

Holding a press conference can be a very quick and effective way of getting significant press coverage and briefing several journalists at a time. But it does require careful consideration because a press conference can be extremely risky. If nothing arouses press interest, the turnout could be poor, and a damp squib may be embarrassing.

Here are some good reasons for holding a press conference:

- To launch your event or conference.
- There is genuine news to impart about someone taking part in the event who is really noteworthy.
- To explain a controversial rumour that has been going round about the event; media speculation can be enormous and damaging.
- To reveal a major exclusive, e.g. that Lord Lucan has been found and he will be the main speaker at the conference.

If a written statement will be adequate, use a press release. To justify a press conference, something has to benefit from further expansion and the appointed spokesperson must be adequately prepared to answer any questions accurately and confidently. Find an easily accessible venue that can provide appropriate hospitality, e.g. performers or artists for a photocall.

Be sure your press conference avoids other major public events and does not clash with major sporting fixtures or arts promotions. Detailed investigation will pay dividends when choosing a date and time. But there is always the danger that a major news story will steal the limelight, and perhaps no one will appear.

It is essential to phone around to remind editors of the invitation already issued and any accompanying information. Try to emphasise that certain people will appear, there will be opportunities for coherent radio and television interviews, and photo opportunities with some novel or unusual performance. Consider who is going to appear in front of the media; a sponsor will often be keen. The chairman of the organising committee or the relevant spokesperson must appear and they must be well briefed.

The venue is very important; hold it somewhere easily covered by journalists. It is important to have media briefings in Manchester, Birmingham, Glasgow or Edinburgh as well as London, but venues outside major cities can cause significant problems. Even on a smaller scale, the main media town in the area is the best launching point.

Assemble the audiovisual aids required for the presentation; a good video or slide show really adds interest. Ensure that investigations go out to journalists well in advance and are followed up by phone calls to individuals who may be interested. Prepare a detailed agenda for the press conference and stick to it, although questions can go on a little longer if the interest exists.

It is also worthwhile to lay on hospitality for journalists and others after the formal part of the press conference. This will allow for informal contact and a slightly different sort of questioning; both can be good for developing relationships.

Photo opportunities

It is very important to create a visual impression as well as a verbal impression. Words are cheap and not necessarily eye-catching, even if they do find space in a newspaper. Yet photographs can attract a great deal of attention. They do take a bit more setting up and a little more imagination, but they can be much more worthwhile. They often generate a greater awareness of your event, so they help to satisfy a sponsor's desire for publicity.

Relevant media

It is essential to involve all the media, not just some. Local radio is an excellent and often forgotten medium. It offers the possibility of announcing events and interviews with organisers. It is also possible to persuade a local radio station to set up its own stand within the event, providing live publicity. Major provincial newspapers or indeed locals can be very important; don't just target the national media.

Your audience's age, interest and likely reading or listening habits will determine which media you particularly want to cultivate. Always remember the special interest press; the UK market is vast. Coverage in the appropriate magazine will be invaluable for ensuring audience support, finding participants and giving nationwide publicity.

A promotional competition (for entry tickets), a discount scheme for bulk attendance or some other type of incentive can be a way to attract interest. Direct marketing through mail or telephone is an extremely effective, if a little intrusive, way of getting the message over to prospective customers. Even for localised events, such word of mouth promotion can be a leading influence in obtaining support.

Public relations

The public handling and public image of the organising group are pivotal component's of a project's success. Public relations policy effectively combines all the relevant issues like advertising, image, logo and media relations with the foremost factors of customer relations and customer care.

Getting a positive image is a high priority for many projects. By their very nature events are often designed to achieve an increased awareness of the activity involved and to create a focal point for interest. Effective public relations is best achieved by influencing people through the influencers. This can be done by using the mass media and by obtaining the support of leading experts in the relevant field. Many people in the arts consider the views of the critics as the deciding factor in gauging success. This may or may not be true, but a recommendation on radio or television can be pivotal to a project's progress. And a celebrity endorsement is often influential. 'There is no such thing as bad publicity' is an old saying. For events, this is not necessarily true; a bad image certainly won't attract spectators, now or in the future. Public relations is the shop window to participants and public; make it as large as possible. It is important to get a good image, but be sure it is justified by good delivery of the project.

Selling

All staff involved in the event have a 'selling' job to do. They need to sell participation in the event as worthwhile to everyone they come in contact with. This means a positive selling approach from the telephonist and the chief executive, as well as everywhere in between. Take every opportunity to interest potential visitors and participants in the project. Everyone in the team becomes a sales representative.

Another aspect to selling takes place at and around the event: merchandising, souvenir sales, franchising and trading. These are the direct financial sales which can make measurable sums of money and contribute massively to event income. For some of the bigger events, franchising (selling all or part sales rights for a fee or percentage) is the most convenient way to produce sales returns without significant work by the organising committee. It is not likely to yield the highest possible return, except in events like the Olympic games. The franchisee gets its share of the profit, partly at the expense of the event organisers. Most often franchised are catering and souvenirs. It may be more appropriate for the organisers to merchandise the goods themselves, realising all possible profits by undertaking all sales.

Event souvenirs and other related sales can be lucrative for any event. They must be carefully considered because the choice of the wrong logo, image or souvenirs can cause a severe financial loss. At all levels, these sales are absolutely vital to financial viability and must be carefully deliberated. Rash decisions can be permanently regretted. It will take courage to venture perhaps limited money on buying goods to resell, but the profits are often a financial lifeline. These sales can also help in conveying an event image for present and future events. A good range of souvenirs will certainly be appreciated; they will remind visitors of a good experience and encourage them to return. A worthwhile investment.

Event presentation

There are two critical aspects:

- the promotional presentation
- the event presentation itself

The promotional presentation is for sponsors, backers, spectators, media and participants. Public expectations are now very high, consumers are used to sophisticated provision by the mass media and most providers in the leisure field. Every effort will be essential to ensure professional and effective presentation of both aspects.

The self-respecting event organiser needs to make a good job of presenting a project to a prospective sponsor or potential participants. This can range from an attractive document, perhaps desktop published, to a high-cost multimedia or audiovisual production. To excite interest, any presentation will need to be accurate, thorough and error-free. Here are some guidelines:

1. Rehearse the presentation.
2. Be well prepared.
3. Double-check all audiovisual equipment, and carry all necessary spares.
4. Ensure written communication is of the highest order.
5. Double-check all materials for factual inaccuracies.
6. Ensure all information is totally correct (e.g. no typing errors).
7. If possible, check out the venue beforehand.
8. Reconfirm the time and place within 24 hours.

Paid or unpaid, only such a professional approach is going to have any chance of succeeding, such are the expectations of the customer. The same meticulous thinking must also be applied to the presentation of the whole event, from beginning to end. This should be an all-encompassing concept. It involves conspicuous items like logos, advertisements, mascots and decor.

Other less obvious elements must also reflect an overall slickness of presentation. If the venture is to be taken seriously by the consumer, then high quality must be the hallmark of everything undertaken and all the event staff who do the work. The project must be accomplished in the correct manner to the highest achievable level, not just completed.

An awareness of how things can appear to the customer should be developed in all staff and volunteers involved. The verbal presentation of guides, officials and speakers will influence how the event is perceived, as will the physical appearance of the venue, its facilities and equipment. Most important will be how the event personnel treat the participants – that is, customer care. A pleasant, positive, caring manner in all dealings will be the most significant aspect of public presentation.

In summary, events marketing involves:

- customer care
- selling
- influencing trends and attitudes
- creating experiences
- research
- segmentation to appropriate areas
- targeting
- entry strategy explaining which level or group to challenge first
- marketing mix of all the P's

Each event should have its own marketing plan that includes these items:

- event aims and objectives
- marketing objectives
- marketing strategy
- environmental and demographic factors
- competition
- specific action through the P's of the marketing mix

Self-assessment questions

1. Identify four P's from the suggested list which you feel to be the most important; state the reasons for your choice.

2. Take the four P's you have identified in Question 1 and consider them in relation to an actual event. Suggest how they affect the event you have chosen, and how they would be 'mixed' by the skilled organiser to ensure a quality event.

3. Choice of media, media relations and advertising are all important. Apply them to a local pop concert and give reasons for the choices you have made and the actions taken.

Chapter Six

Event Evaluation

It is vital that each and every event, large or small, has an extensive evaluation process. This should be carried out at the end (summative) as well as considered throughout the event (formative). During the project development, this process is usually termed controlling or monitoring, but really it is an ongoing evaluation of success. Such control mechanisms will be essential all the way, to ensure that expenditure and action are on target and up to schedule.

Responsibility for this monitoring process should be allocated to appropriate individuals or groups, but must also be seen as the joint responsibility of everyone in the organisation. The mechanics of this control may be a formal financial audit or an informal chat between colleagues. Best of all, a good evaluation process should really utilise all possible methods to ensure the project remains focused.

The end evaluation is equally vital and should be carried out on each and every occasion. The degree of formality will vary between situations, ranging from a few questionnaires to professionally canvassed market research, and from a discussion between two colleagues to a wide-ranging cascade of debriefing sessions for all levels of staff. Although the mechanics may vary, the principle is the same; end evaluation is vital and must be carried out.

It is important to have some criteria for the event evaluation. Hard criteria concern the outputs; they tend to be tangible and quantitative. Soft criteria concern the process; they tend to be intangible and qualitative.

Hard criteria

- deadlines
- cost requirements
- performance specifications
- resource constraints
- specific quality standards

Soft criteria

- a cooperative attitude
- total quality
- a positive image
- ethical conduct .
- staff commitment

SMART objectives

Ultimately, though, any event must be judged against its own set of SMART objectives. Remember, they have been chosen to be specific, measurable and timed, so it must be possible to assess the event against them (otherwise they are probably the wrong objectives or they are incorrectly stated). The objectives for a local arts festival could include these:

- To increase event attendance by 10% over last year.
- To increase the number of performers by 5% overall and provide two new-style programmes
- To establish one new performing arts group in the area within three months of the festival.

All of these objectives are measurable and can be quite clearly evaluated to gauge success or failure in achieving them. This will then allow considered analysis of the end facts and the event's overall success, measured against these objectives. Here are some possible methods for obtaining the necessary information:

- statistics, e.g. attendances, participants
- financial returns
- questionnaires for participants, VIPs, etc.
- customer focus groups
- staff discussions
- detailed interviews
- exit surveys
- formal meetings
- external consultant opinion

The choice of method will depend on the specific event scale and complexity. Always remember others, like local colleges, may be quite happy to help in this process. And remember the fifteen C's of event evaluation:

Compulsory It must be done for every event, large or small

Concise It should be no longer than necessary.

Concurrent It should take place during the event and continue after it.

Constant Throughout the event and even in the earlier planning stages, consider how to evaluate success. Evaluation should take place all the time.

Customised Although there may be an existing checklist for evaluation, each project should have an additional set of criteria to match its own unique objectives.

Consulted Evaluation involves seeking the opinions of as many relevant groups as possible, e.g. participants, officials, VIPs, sponsors.

Canvassed Canvass opinion, do not wait for it to be given; just because customers don't actively complain, it doesn't mean they're happy.

Circulated Circulate among people to gather opinions; circulate the debrief document as widely as possible, to help everyone involved build for the future.

Customer focused Whatever the nature of the customers, they must all be asked for an evaluation through means like exit surveys.

Colleague based All staff, paid or voluntary, should be involved in evaluating their part within the event.

Collected Care should be taken to collect appropriate information.

Catalogued Record information in an appropriate way and file it for future reference.

Complete It should cover all aspects of the event from before arrival to after departure.

Communicated It should be communicated to all relevant parties, explaining how the debrief is conducted and reporting its findings.

Copied Successful evaluation methods should be reused on future projects in order to repeat their success.

Self-assessment questions

1. During events, controlling and monitoring are vitally important to ensure focused and measured progress. As event organiser for a young people's week-long international conference, what mechanisms and procedures would you put in place to achieve these processes?

2. After the conference you have to carry out an effective evaluation to determine whether the event was a success and whether it should be held again next year. What precise steps would you take and why?

Chapter Seven

Practical Event Management

This chapter describes some examples of event organisation, along with devices and procedures for practical implementation. The first six chapters have outlined the managerial, organisational and financial structures to be considered. This chapter illustrates how the process is achieved, giving case studies and methods actually used by professionals.

The accompanying documents are drawn from a variety of sources; many of them I devised myself, others have been produced by people operating in the field. All are appropriately acknowledged, but sincere thanks must go to each individual and organisation for allowing their work to be published to assist colleagues and students in the pursuit of excellence for event provision. This chapter aims to cite good practice and to give those working in events actual documents they could usefully adapt to their own situation.

Bude Jazz Festival

This section is about an arts event in the West Country, England's West Country and Britain's number one holiday destination, where tourism is estimated to be worth in excess of £2.2 billion a year. Bude is a seaside resort on the coast of north Cornwall, popular with families and surfers. Businesses in this Victorian town are small and family run, typical of most tourism in the West Country. Tourism is the main industry in Bude and the trade there is mainly domestic, with over 95% of all trips into Cornwall made by Britons. In the last fifteen years the trends in Bude have broadly matched other regional and national trends and, in recent years, there has been a recovery and a stabilising of visit figures.

Bude is the home of the Bude Jazz Festival. Visitors to the Jazz Festival can buy stroller tickets. The holder of a stroller ticket, at any time of the day from midday to midnight, has access to jazz in some or all of the stroller venues in the town. For an extra charge there are special evening extras, either big-name bands or newly commissioned shows. There are four New Orleans street parades and a Bude Jazz Festival church service.

The festival starts on August bank holiday and runs through the following week and weekend. The festival was started in 1988 by a one-man agency, Jazz Arts and Directions, based in Birmingham. The organisation of the festival was shared with North Cornwall Arts, an association which promotes and encourages the arts in north Cornwall and whose funders include South West Arts, local authorities and charitable trusts.

Since 1988 the number of jazz sessions, the number of visitors to the festival and the budget have risen steadily. In 1990 there were 7000 attendances over the eight days of the festival and in 1992 there was an estimated budget of over £50,000 providing 150 predominately traditional jazz events, 70 bands and star guests, and performances in 25 venues in Bude and very nearby. It was confidently expected that over 80% of those who attended would be from outside Bude and the immediate area.

The marketing plan takes up just under 10% of the overall budget and includes a poster, leaflets and bought advertising. It also includes advertisement swapping with other jazz festivals that run a programme of cooperative promotion. There is an increasing use of direct mail as attendees to the festival increase, and there is a press and public relations programme.

Support for the festival has come in small amounts of sponsorship and grants, and in other forms. The highest amount of sponsorship was £750 and the district council has given some financial assistance. The town council has provided an office, merchandising space in the town during the festival, the free use of the town's main hall for three of the evening events, and a small grant.

The West Country Tourist Board has given support with financial assistance from its Special Promotions Fund. This, in common with all regional boards, is developed by the English Tourist Board; the fund is £2500 for the six counties of the West Country for the whole year. Nonetheless, it is possible from that to give significant help in the early days to perhaps ten new and important events in the region. The Bude Jazz Festival has received assistance from the Special Promotions Fund, partly because it has proved to be so appropriate to the location, but equally because there is considerable evidence that members of the West Country Tourist Board whose businesses are in Bude support the principles of the festival.

The tourist trade is generally supportive. In the first year there was a hard core of hoteliers who were sympathetic to the idea of hosting jazz sessions in their premises, but a major problem for the organisers was to find enough venues. Now, three years later, that is markedly easier.

The demands from potential hosts of the music now more nearly match the available supply. The organiser has to draw a balance between rewarding the hoteliers who have been loyal from the very beginning and encouraging new and potential venues. There are the stroller venues – hotels, pubs, clubs, restaurants and a holiday park. They pay between £40 and £80 to stage a stroller session, and this income now contributes about 25% of the total costs of all artists fees and staging. A broader range of accommodation can support the festival by advertising on the reverse side of the leaflet. In fact, this funds the main flyer advertisement leaflet. Those are some examples of how the tourist trade gets involved in a practical way with the festival.

What Bude Jazz Festival has proved is that one person with support can run a big one-off event with success. It has focused the attention and the energies of people onto the already busy August bank holiday, but more important, through the following week, which has traditionally been much less busy, and particularly onto the weekend following that. The time of year must now stay the same; Bude has its own niche in the festival calendar and it certainly shouldn't try to take on and beat a similar existing event. There is now an idea in the town for a Spring festival, to feature jazz and then to extend perhaps to theatre and art. That is a big idea and it will be lovely if it happens, but it needs a backer.

Current successful activity includes Bude Jazz Breaks, special weekends organised by Jazz Arts and Directions. A small hotel underwrites the event and engages the Bude Jazz Festival organiser as agent for the bands playing and as a publicist for the event.

The links between tourism and the arts are recognised and are being formally drafted in a West Country Tourist Board and South West Arts joint policy statement. One of the concerns of the statement is to look at ways in which events that patently increase tourism can be encouraged and promoted. The Bude Jazz Festival is obviously such an event – it clearly increases tourism spend in the town of Bude. Here are some of the lessons from the Bude Jazz Festival:

- The strength of the festival and the Jazz Breaks promotion is that both are based on people doing what they are best at.
- The strength of the festival is that the organiser, the hotels and the venues have stayed with each other and have stayed with the idea.
- Support from North Cornwall Arts and from the trade has been much more important than any sponsorship.
- It is important to match the character of the town or resort with the entertainment, the art or the music.
- It is best to establish a group or consortium of the tourist trade, local art venues and the local arts associations; do that right at the very beginning.

The above section is a rough transcript of a presentation made to an Arts Council seminar by Nigel Buckler of the West Country Tourist Board.

The Great North Run

This section is about the Great North Run, and it concentrates on 1988. The event is too complex to give full details, but this overview should contain relevant information.

Facts and figures

Basic details

Originator	Brendan Foster
Idea for event	Based upon Round the Bays Race, New Zealand
Distance	13 miles 192½ yards
Inaugural year	1981
Route	Linear
Start	Newcastle Town Moor (Central Motorway)
Finish	South Shields, The Leas
Status	National AAA and BSAD Half-Marathon Championships
	AAA = Amateur Athletic Association
	BSAD = British Sports Association for Disabled

1988 committee structure

Nova International Ltd (Events Division)

Chairman	Brendan Foster
Race director	John Caine
Start director	Dave Roberts
Finish director	Allan Wilson
Course director and coordinator	Max Coleby

Administration and finance

Accountant	George McCowie
Finance director	Jennifer Moxon
Secretary	Cherry Alexander
Processing of entries	Jo Anderson (based at South Shields)

Jo Anderson was assisted by a team of two to eight helpers, depending on demand. The structure of the working relationship which exists within the organisation of the Great North Run can be more clearly seen in a later diagram (p. 83). Note how the work is divided into individual areas beneath each section head. This outlines the personnel structure of how that particular aspect of the event is organised.

Computer services

The Treasurer's Department of Newcastle City Council is responsible for registration of entrants and production of results. The Great North Run is a unique event in that each entrant is allocated their own finishing position and time, made possible by computype bar codes on each number which are read and processed at the end of the race using MSI equipment.

Time to load bar codes on to computer	12 hours
Time to process and finalise results	3 days

Race personnel (excluding police, medical and communications personnel)

Start	80
Route feed stations	168
Finish	410
Total	658

Communication points (Royal Signals Troop, Catterick Garrison)

Start	3
Route	11
Finish	1

Major medical points

- start
- 10-mile point
- finish

Growth of the event

Year	Entries	Finishers
1981	12,000	10,677
1982	19,000	18,284
1983	21,000	19,339
1984	25,000	24,183
1985	27,000	23,848
1986	27,000	25,023
1987	27,000	25,737
1988	27,000	25,316
1989	limit raised to 30,000	

Miscellaneous details

Age limit	17 and over
Entry fee (1988)	£6.25 club members
	£6.75 non-members

Each successful participant receives
- race number and bar code
- certificate with calculated position and time
- car sticker
- information leaflet
- T-shirt
- medal
- refreshments during and after race

All profits from all festival events go into the Registered Great North Charitable Trust Fund. Approximately two hundred elite athletes receive appearance money for their trust fund.

Fastest time	60 min 43 s (Mike Musyoki, world record)
Average time, men	1 h 45 min
Average time, women	2 h 24 min

Sponsorship

Alan Pascoe Associates (APA) are the sole marketing agents for British Athletics and were appointed by the Amateur Athletics Association and the British Amateur Athletics Board. Their responsibilities include negotiating television coverage for all domestic athletics events, finding and negotiating sponsorship. The main sponsor for the Great North Run 1986–1989 was Pearl Assurance PLC, who provided:

- financial support
- public liability insurance
- VIP marquee, supplies and services
- route bannering at 24 locations along the route

Minor sponsors and supporters of the event provide additional necessary services and equipment. Their association with the event accounts for 41 further route bannering locations. Details of these organisations are given in Table 7.1.

Marketing and promotion

The marketing and promotion of the Great North Run are now greatly assisted by its size and the emergence of other festival events. The Festival of Sport creates publicity from its reputation alone; it is in the interests of the press and other media to cover these events, which cumulatively involve thousands of people. Nevertheless, it is important that an event creates the right image, which will generate even greater support.

The event logo is an important base from which the image of the event is developed. The Festival of Sport was inaugurated in 1988 and the special logo illustrates the vibrant message and cheerful optimism which the organisers sought to create during the week's events. The event largely relies on the field of elite athletes, and disclosing their names generates many items of news, which further publicise the event. And if the organisers can attract a particularly high-calibre field, who subsequently record fast times, this attracts further attention to the event, which in turn guarantees future sponsorship and television support. This situation was achieved in 1986 when Mike Musyoki broke the world record.

Organisation	Contribution and main responsibilities
Presto Foods and Argyle Stores	40,000 flavoured drinks 170,000 Tetra packs of water for feed stations Transports facilities, e.g. T-shirts, refreshments
Newcastle Chronicle and Journal Ltd	Publicity and promotion of event Publishing of entry forms Normal daily circulation 60,000–70,000 copies Application form edition, 120,000 copies
British Red Cross and St John Ambulance	All medical personnel and equipment for first-aid stations
Royal Signals (Catterick Garrison)	Communications network
AAA race officials	Race starting and officiating
AA	Traffic diversion signs
District Councils Newcastle City Council Gateshead MBC Borough of South Tyneside	Barriers, cones, etc. Construction of start and finish areas Road closures in conjunction with the police Cleaning after the event
TBS	Official Great North Run training shoe suppliers
Northumbria Police	Close and open roads according to prearranged timetable and progress of runners Liaison with race organisers about casualties Marshal traffic and spectators
Metro Radio	Official Great North Festival of Sport Radio Station Publicity and promotion of event* Population = 1,430,000 Weekly audience = 687,000 Percentage reach of all adults = 48% Average hours listened = 13.6
ITV Sport	Televising the event (national coverage seen by 3 million viewers)

* Data from RSGB survey.

Table 7.1:
Organisations involved in the 1988 Great North Run

Venue management

There are enormous demands on the start and finish systems throughout the day. These are key areas to address.

The start

- Construction of the start system begins at 3.30 am on the morning of the event and both carriageways of the motorway are closed until the clean-up operation has finished at around 12 noon.

- The whole start system for 27,000 runners occupies roughly half a mile of motorway.

- Each pair of dummy lamp columns denotes 1000 runners and bannering has to be erected to direct competitors to their respective start sections.
- Important provision is given to roadside banner advertising for the sponsors.
- A large area of the town moor is required in addition to the motorway and this accommodates toilet marquees, a 200-yard latrine, information huts, PA cabin and space for television vehicles.
- Twenty-seven double-decker buses (marked alphabetically) transport competitors baggage to South Shields. They are situated behind the start and leave half an hour before the main event in order to arrive at the finish before the competitors.
- Note the importance of the lead car, with the large race clock, for the benefit of the spectators as well as the elite athletes.
- Imagine what 27,000 runners look like as they stream across the starting line. This highlights the scale of the event and the need for large amounts of event equipment and services (e.g. toilets and a PA system).

The finish

- Construction for the finish system begins five days before the actual event.
- Note the large space required to accommodate all activities associated with the finish.
- The organisers are fully aware of problems associated with bottlenecks of runners; they avoid bottlenecks by drawing the runners through the following finish process:
  1. Collect bar code from number.
  2. Collect medal.
  3. Collect T-shirt.
  4. Collect drink.
  5. Collect baggage from allocated bus.
- By planning the finish system like this, the runners are relatively unaware that they have been drawn some 600 yards away from the finish line. This avoids the runners converging upon, and interfering with, the immediate finish line.
- The actual finish line which has four colour-coded crossing points, feeds six funnels for the collection of bar codes and the monitoring of individual times.
- The funnel system before the race will be finalised once the scale of provision has been ascertained. The construction of the start and finish systems involves over 1700 metres of crowd control barriers, 1500 metres of chestnut fencing, 5500 metres of rope and 1100 wooden stakes.
- Notice the positioning of the television cameras and note the amusement activities which take place on the day. Attention is not only given to catering for the runners but also the numerous spectators.
- Look at the size of the finish operation, especially the huge volume of refreshments required, together with the T-shirt collection points further ahead and the long line of baggage buses.
- The construction of a feed station can only take place once the roads are completely closed. Each station requires roughly between fourteen and twenty-four staff, and refreshments are staggered on each side of the road. A Presto lorry transports various event materials, as well as advertising its name.

Why is the event so successful?

After organising the event for eight years, clear patterns and norms have become established. The operation of the event is now so well rehearsed and understood by all concerned, its success is guaranteed. The following points can be identified in contributing to this success, which is not entirely down to the management style:

- The nature of the Geordie public.
- The perceived value of the event; competitors are happy with what they receive in return for the entry fee.
- The positive image of the event itself – belonging to the group.
- The growth in popularity of running – a fad of the day.
- People see it as a way of getting fit, so they are happy to adopt a training schedule and stick to it.
- The success of the publicity and promotional vehicle, boosted by the quality of the BBC television coverage during the early years.
- The ability of the organisers to evaluate, modify and better the event each successive year.
- It is 'a good day out for all'.

This event profile was prepared by Nigel Gough of Nova International Ltd, Newcastle upon Tyne, who kindly agreed to its publication.

Tall Ships Australia

The Tall Ships 1988 event in Melbourne has been described as the biggest single event ever staged in Victoria and an outstanding success from all aspects. Tall Ships as a spectacle appealed to Victorians on several levels. It evoked a deep and universal love of the sea and stirred half-forgotten cultural memories of a time when Australia had depended on it for everything. Perhaps more poignantly, it reminded Australians how responsibility passes down the generations and alerted them to the needs of the young.

The Tall Ships national director, Rear Admiral Rothesay Swan, has captured the essence:

> *What better adventure and challenge could a young person possibly have than to conquer the unpredictable oceans aboard a magnificent Tall Ship? And what an exciting way to establish friendships between nations and their peoples, where hundreds of miles from land, a common goal becomes a common bond.*

In keeping with this spirit, hundreds of enthusiastic volunteers joined the team on Princes Pier, Port Melbourne, to enable 1.5 million visitors to experience the magic of tall ships and the opening celebrations of Australia's bicentennial year led by the prime minister.

Tall Ships: some background

The first tall ships event in 1956, a race from Torbay, England to Lisbon, Portugal, drew ships from five nations and was billed as a last hurrah for the square-riggers. However, it caught the imagination of everyone involved and became instead thé first event of the new era of tall ships. Tall Ships Australia 1988 was historically important in that it was the first tall ships event held in the southern hemisphere and demanded that participating vessels from overseas made the longest and most dangerous voyage in the 32-year history of tall ships racing.

Definition of a tall ship

Contrary to some media-led public expectations, not all tall ships are giant square-riggers. The term *tall ships* is used to define single-hull sailing vessels with a minimum waterline length of 30 ft (9.14 m) engaged in sailing training and carrying a crew comprising 50% sail trainees aged between 16 and 25 years. Sail trainees are defined as young men and women training as future officers or ratings in either naval or mercantile services, or young people who are given experience in deepwater sailing vessels as part of their education or personal development programme.

Tall ships are divided into three classes:

Class A fully rigged ships
All square-rigged vessels
Fore and aft rigged vessels of 48.8 m (160 ft and over)

Class B Fore and aft rigged vessels 30.5–48.8 m (100–160 ft)

Class C All fore and aft rigged vessels from 9.14 m (30 ft) LWL
LWL = low-water level

Management structure

The overall project was conceived and directed at a national level from the Australian Bicentennial Authority (ABA) headquarters in Sydney, but the actual organisation and administration of the event in each state was carried out at a local level (Fig. 7.1). This case study is for Melbourne, Victoria. For the purpose of delineating operations specific to either national or state budgets, events were described as either 'on the pier' or 'shoreside'. In practice it was all one event with all services and activities designed and coordinated to cater for the same audience of visitors and crews.

Group roles

Administration committee
This committee mushroomed into a complex infrastructure, which not only provided a comprehensive array of services and facilities on the pier, but coordinated the administration of all services, facilities and offices. The group was tasked with the following responsibilities:

- administration
- vessels
- crew
- public
- event
- general

Although presented only in point form under each of these headings, the detailed requirements of each section will convey the complexity and breadth of organisation to enable the Tall Ships visit to take place successfully.

Administration Responsibility was held for the overall administration of the Tall Ships event in Melbourne, including budgetary control and provision of all facilities and support services for the following offices and units:

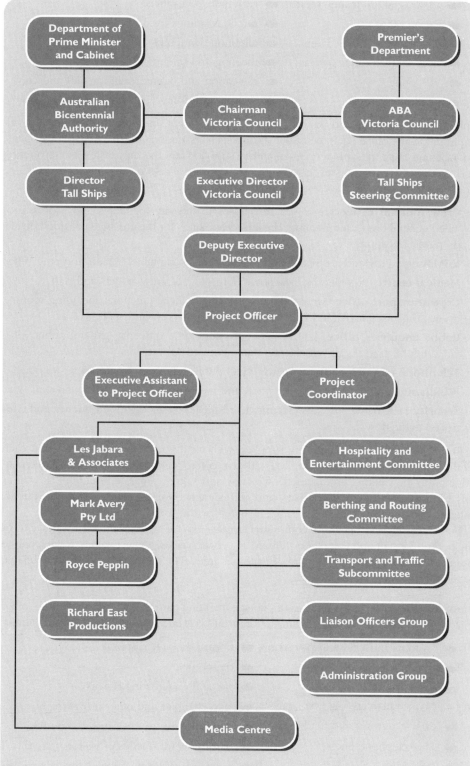

Figure 7.1
The management
structure for Tall
Ships 1988

(Reproduced courtesy of Earle Bloomfield)

- administration headquarters
- liaison office
- director's office
- crew tourism office
- VIP lounge
- medical centre
- crew transport office
- public enquiries caravan
- telephone enquiries office
- meeting and briefing area
- recreation and dining room for staff and crew
- security task force

This included cleaning and painting offices, laying carpet, installing telephones, providing furniture and office equipment such as desks, chairs, cupboards, shelving, photocopiers, fax machines, and all stationery and ancillary supplies. Another key task was the printing and issuing of security passes, car parking passes, pier access passes and food vouchers. The roles of the above offices are summarised as follows:

Crew tourism office Organised free buses to the city for crews and cadets; provided general tourist information, organised bookings for theatre, etc.; provided details on public transport, etc.

VIP lounge Provided hospitality and refreshments to captains, officers and other VIPs.

Medical centre Provided medical services to officers, crew, cadets and staff.

Crew transport office Arranged transport for all official functions, including sporting events; organised taxis (and water taxis) for officers, crew and staff.

Public enquiries office Acted as central information office for general public; provided information on all vessels, entertainment and ABA events.

Telephone enquiries office Answered all public telephone enquiries.

Windjammer club Provided recreation and meals for all crew, cadets and staff.

Security task force Provided security to restricted areas; organised queues and controlled traffic flow.

Staff and volunteers were not only supplied with meal vouchers for all meals, but each of the above offices was also supplied with tea, coffee, cold drinks, biscuit and cakes. In addition to the catering arrangements for crew and staff, a separate restaurant as well as an extensive variety of snack bars and refreshments were organised for the public. Internal communications were greatly enhanced by the use of mobile cellphones.

Before operations began, a comprehensive handbook was produced by the city of Melbourne for staff and volunteers. It listed all services, rules, contact names and telephone numbers, office responsibilities and operational times. The handbook was made available to all staff working on the project.

Vessels In addition to the services of pilotage, berthing parties, tugs, etc., there were other vital requirements which the administration group became responsible for coordinating:

- Customs and Excise inspections
- quarantine of ship waste
- provision of charts and navigational aids
- extra gangways and fenders
- ship telephone lines
- ship water
- power
- normal garbage disposal
- diesel fuel
- sail and engineering repairs
- ship chandler and other providers
- daily supplies of fresh bread and milk
- barricades for queues of visitors
- noticeboards listing opening times of vessels
- loudhailers to announce opening times

Lines of power cable and light bulbs could be loaned out to vessels for dressing them at night. They were not provided in Melbourne, but many vessels had none of their own. The enhanced nightly spectacle would have been worth the cost, and a sponsor could almost certainly have been found.

Crew and cadets   Living for an extended period aboard ship, whether as a cadet or a professional sailor, develops a need to get away and perhaps find some outside stimulation, privacy and a homely environment, besides the more practical needs of overseas travellers. These facilities were provided on Princes Pier:

- first-class extensive showers and toilets
- laundry and dry-cleaning service
- medical centre, fully staffed, with daily sick parade
- post office
- bank with money-changing facility
- local and ISD telephones
- recreation room with lounge, table tennis, television, games, etc.
- Restaurant and Heineken bar (the Windjammer Club)
- interpreter service
- free public transport
- free water taxis
- free Commonwealth cars and buses for captains, officers and crew
- tourist information and theatre-booking service
- concerts, sports and other entertainment
- free coach tours organised by Victour to major tourist destinations

The restaurant and bar was open from 0730 to 2400. Tea, coffee and biscuits were provided free of charge and meals were greatly subsidised for disadvantaged cadets through provision of meal vouchers. Staff were drawn from local ethnic groups matched to the visiting ships.

In future it is recommended that more time should be spent to ensure cadets receive free food and travel, passes to cinemas, discos, art galleries and museums, free or subsidised airfares within Australia, vouchers for selected restaurants, and invitations or free tickets to sporting events.

The public   Although the crew benefited from the relative isolation of their first-floor facilities, it often meant some duplication to provide adequately for the general public, whose numbers could only be guessed at before the event. The following facilities and services were provided for the public:

- food outlets, including a restaurant and normal fast-food stands
- drinks, hot and cold, including beer booths
- souvenir stalls with a predominant Tall Ships theme
- mobile medical and first-aid services
- toilets, including disabled rooms
- ramps and other disabled facilities
- public telephones

- banking facilities
- post office selling first-day covers, stamps, etc.
- public car parking
- crowd control staff, mobile and radio connected
- public transport collection and drop-off points
- lost children's room
- nursing mothers and young families rooms
- information booths distributing general bicentennial and Tall Ships, material
- noticeboards listing information on vessel opening times, berthing plan and events programme
- public seating and sheltered areas
- telephone enquiries and information, recorded and live
- extensive public entertainment programme

Crowd control emerged as the most important matter, requiring an alert yet sensitive team with relevant experience and a properly thought-out emergency plan. Lifeguards in inflatable boats patrolled beneath the pier for anyone unlucky enough to fall off.

More shaded and seating areas for the public shoreside could have been provided as the site was bereft of any shelter whatsoever. The post office proved incredibly popular. There were constantly long queues waiting for first-day covers and franking of stamps. Pedestrian traffic flow dutifully filed along the pier in the hoped for anticlockwise direction, emerging through the exit gate after an average of $1\frac{1}{2}$ hours of quiet and orderly strolling and visiting the various ships.

The official number of spectators over the period was reported to be 1.5 million, the largest single event ever staged in Victoria.

Event The following checklist was used for the Melbourne operation:

- security (24 hours) for vessels and pier facilities
- daily cleaning in toilets, offices, recreation and dining room and on concourse
- rubbish removal
- crowd control
- insurance – public liability
            – event
            – marine insurance assessor (24 hours)
- decorations (posters, bunting, banners)
- signage
- lighting
- barricades
- security passes for vehicles and personnel
- car parking and passes
- vehicle access – emergency
               – taxis
               – VIP transport
               – crew buses

        – disabled cars and buses
        – service vehicles
        – rubbish collection
        – toilet waste

- police
- fire brigade
- ambulance service
- medical and first-aid service
- publicity
- council requirements
- power
- water
- emergency repair service
- catering
- toilets
- taxis
- public transport
- water transport and taxis
- public address system

Berthing and routing committee

It was the responsibility of this committee to get the fleet safely through the heads and berthed at Princes Pier, then out again in an orderly procession past the governor's barge and safely through the heads in Port Phillip bay. The task called for a wide range of skills and brought together representatives from the following organisations:

- Port Phillip Sea Pilots
- Company of Master Mariners
- Port of Melbourne Authority
- Union Bulkships
- Royal Australian Navy
- Williamstown Naval Dockyard
- Royal Yacht Club of Victoria
- Marine Board of Victoria
- Victoria Police – Water Police
- Melbourne Tug Service

The overall task was broken down into the following phases:

1. Development of a master routing plan and emergency procedure plan.
2. Design and construction of a C class marina attached to Princes Pier, together with emergency berthing alternatives for stormy weather.
3. Arrangement for berthing, including tugs, lines boats and shore parties.
4. Plans for the final parade of sail, for the governor to take the salute.
5. Anchorage plan for overnight stay in Capel Sound, off Rye, before arrival at Princes Pier.
6. Arrangements to ensure safety of all spectator vessels during movements of fleet.

As was to be expected from such a strong and professional committee, all berthing and routing movements went without a hitch. Of all the participating organisations, only the Port of Melbourne Authority made any charge for services provided, and then only at cost.

Hospitality and entertainment committee

Through subcommittees and work groups, this committee had responsibility for organising the following items.

Official reception (31 December 1987, 1800–2000) Principally organised to welcome the Tall Ships crews to Victoria, the function was attended by almost 3000 people. Guests were welcomed by the premier of Victoria and addressed by the prime minister. The venue chosen was the Customs Hall, Inner Terminal, Station Pier. Musical entertainment was provided.

Captains' dinner (31 December 1987, 2000–2400) The traditional captains' dinner was designed to specially recognise all Tall Ships captains and introduce them to Victoria. The function was attended by 450 people. Guests were welcomed by the chairman of the Tall Ships Steering Committee, Mr John Bertrand, and addressed by both the premier of Victoria and the prime minister. The captain of Spain's Tall Ship, the *Juan Sebastian de Elcano*, proposed the toast to Australia. The entertainment consisted of music and dancing. The function was held in the TT Lines Departure Lounge, adjacent to the reception venue.

Sightseeing tours In conjunction with Victour, coach and rail tours were provided to visit some of Victoria's most popular tourist destinations. The tours were free of charge and crews were able to mix freely with the paying public, who filled up the vacant seats. If anything, the tours were oversubscribed and reports confirmed their popularity. The tour destinations were

- Sovereign Hill Gold Mining Town, Ballarat
- Goulburn River, Mitchelton Winery Cruise
- Coal Creek Historic Village, Korumburra
- Penguin Parade, Phillip Island
- Billa Billa Homestead and Healsville Wildlife Sanctuary
- Puffing Billy Steam Train, Dandenongs
- Melbourne, City Sights Tour
- Shipwreck Coast, Warrnambool

There were up to seven departures on each of the three days that tours were arranged. All meals and entrance fees were provided cost-free by Victour and facility managers.

Civic receptions Receptions were given by Melbourne, South Melbourne, Port Melbourne and St Kilda City Councils. They were coordinated so as to minimise conflicting schedules.

Cultural groups Participation of various ethnic and cultural groups in welcoming and departure ceremonies, and in providing home visits and functions was encouraged and accommodated.

Special events The committee also initially oversaw public entertainment events which Les Jabara & Associates were responsible for organising:

- opening fireworks display
- aerobatic and paraglider displays
- Royal Australian Naval Band performances
- concert stage performances

- welcome celebrations as Tall Ships docked
- departure ceremonies and daylight fireworks

As the event drew closer, much of the overseeing and coordinating needed to be centralised within the office of the project officer.

Liaison officers group

The liaison officers acted as the vital interface between the fleet and crews, and the extensive facilities and entertainment provided for them. The group was established under the leadership of a chief liaison officer and two deputies. Once fully briefed on their task, they recruited and trained more than one hundred officers, drawing on Naval cadets, yacht clubs, Scouts, Guides and the Royal Australian Naval Reserve.

A comprehensive handbook was produced to enable each officer to help his or her tall ship with anything from salvage divers and ship chandlers to late-night shopping and limousine hire. Each tall ship was assigned a liaison officer and an assistant. This ensured that adequate contact between ship and shore could be maintained at all times. In the case of larger foreign vessels officially representing their governments, a Royal Australian Naval Officer was appointed as liaison officer for the duration of the voyage in Australian waters.

There was an abundance of liaison officers and those not able to get their own ship were assigned other duties, helping in one of the many crew service facilities. The liaison office was open 24 hours per day, with Royal Australian Naval personnel working through the small hours. The chief and deputy chief liaison officers attended the project officer's early morning briefing for all section leaders at 0700. This was followed at 0730 by a full briefing to all liaison officers who were, in turn, expected to be aboard their respective vessels by 0800 to brief the crew for the day's special events. Where a major part of any crew were joining one of the tours, either the liaison officer or the assistant would accompany them as guide.

In the case of functions held by individual ships, a separate liaison officer was appointed to coordinate everything from security railing and VIP transport to the delivery of fresh oysters. In particular, the liaison office performed an important role in maintaining information flow, especially to the media office.

In preparation for the fleet's arrival through the heads on 30 December, many officers had begun to monitor the progress of the vessels. Some vessels had arrived a few days early and were berthed upriver; others anchored at Queenscliff, having come through the heads the previous night. Those still in Bass Strait were tracked on VHF and SSB radio and through the Federal Sea Safety and Surveillance Centre in Canberra.

The liaison office displayed huge whiteboards with all vessels and their details well marked, while position charts were constantly altered and the details telephoned or radioed through to the media office. Vessels arriving late or leaving early were also checked through this office. In addition, all mail and messages were handled here. This was especially important in assisting crew changes with overseas vessels (organising air tickets, departure tax, and transport to and from the airport).

Media centre

Originally proposed to occupy a site on the pier, the media centre was moved shoreside to occupy the offices of the Victorian Rock Foundation. These offices were almost fully equipped with desks, chairs, typewriters and had telex, fax and telephones. Additional typewriters and another large fax machine were installed. Mobile cellphones were also used extensively, some by senior media staff of the Australian Bicentennial Authority (ABA) and some by journalists. The centre was also supplied with cold drinks, coffee and tea.

One room was set up as a radio interview room, and the central office space was converted to act as a media briefing area and a television interview stage. The centre was usually open from 0700 until 2100, and sometimes as late as 2300. Staffing required both national and local involvement. A senior ABA media consultant and their assistant, who travelled from point to point with the fleet, were on hand to advise the state ABA media manager. These staff were supported by telex and fax operators, typists and receptionists, managed by the principals of Les Jabara & Associates.

Possibly the most important factor to arise in maintaining information flow was the strong link established with the liaison office. The liaison office extended its role to that of newshound, chasing stories and information on request as well as providing regular updates to the media centre.

Transport and traffic subcommittee

This subcommittee was given the task of developing an overall traffic movement strategy plan in conjunction with the following bodies:

- The City of Port Melbourne
- The City of Melbourne
- The City of St Kilda
- The City of South Melbourne
- The Metropolitan Transit Authority
- V/Line
- Independent busline operators
- Independent taxi cab operators
- Victoria Police
- Fire brigade, ambulance and other emergency services

Their planning included several specific areas:

- Closure of the operations area surrounding Princes Pier Tall Ships site.
- Policing of closed or restricted areas.
- Movement of general public into and out of event area by bus, rail, tram, taxi and private car.
- Special late-night provisions for New Year's Eve.
- Creation of emergency vehicle routes.

Predictions of crowd size ranged from half a million to three million, which left the subcommittee feeling as though they were shadow boxing when they were planning. That things went as well as they did is a great credit to their comprehensive work and their commitment to the task.

Onshore programme: event management contractors

Les Jabara & Associates were appointed by the steering committee to provide and manage the overall shoreside programme. This covered the following areas:

- concessions for food and entertainment
- supply of essential services
- car parking and vehicle movement control
- liaison with police and emergency services
- security
- coordination of entertainment and special events
  - fireworks
  - aerobatic displays

    – skydivers
    – woodchopping championships
- provision of entertainment
    – official reception
    – 'captains' dinner
    – the two concert stages
- set-up and administration of the media centre

Recognised experts were appointed by Jabara to handle each specialist area:

- Mark Avery Pty Ltd
    – vehicle and pedestrian traffic flow
    – police and emergency services
    – security control
    – concession administration
    – public toilets
- Richard East Productions
    – produced, staged and mounted the New Year's Eve concert
    – managed stage daily for performances during the event
    – erected stage and fencing
    – supplied seating and grandstand
    – supplied all technical equipment
    – organised catering for artists
- Entertainment Sound Protection
    – security guards and patrols
- Royce Peppin
    – selection of concession holders
    – negotiation of rates payable to the ABA Victoria Council

Les Jabara & Associates planned to use a large area of vacant land opposite Princes Pier to accommodate circuses, carnivals, concessions and bush-style entertainment. And two large buildings were to have housed ambitious displays depicting Australia's civilian and military history.

The land, a formal petroleum storage site, was being acquired for a housing development. At the last moment of event planning, the Environment Protection Authority declared the area off limits due to soil contamination. This left a roadway and a selection of railway easement – far less space to cater for an expected crowd of over one million. Jabara trimmed the plans to suit and managed well. The remaining concession holders did a brisk trade.

Summary

The whole event was successful if measured by the number of people who attended the pier and environs. But here are some ways it could have been improved:

- Ensure major entertainment does not detract from the ships themselves. It is possible that the main stage made access more difficult than it needed to be.
- Explain in simpler terms the concept of tall ships so the public know what to expect.
- Integrate the whole event so there is no potential disharmony between pier and shoreside activity organisers.
- Maintain an efficient multiperson and information access system for the public.

The above section is included by permission of Earle Bloomfield, former Tall Ships project director and now managing director of Kidsplay Limited in Exeter.

Leisurelend

Originally launched by Gordon District Council (now replaced by Aberdeenshire Council) in the north of Scotland, Leisurelend loans out a variety of special equipment along with appropriate parts lists and instructions. The service has been running since 1991 and has proved popular with community event organisers.

Reference	Item
1	Competitors' race numbers: 2 sets 1–300 in yellow PVC and safety pins
2	Shoulder numbers: 3 sets 1–50 in fluorescent yellow and orange PVC
3	Official bibs: 24 in fluorescent yellow PVC
4	Banners with attached hanging ropes: 1 start, 1 finish and 1 starter's chequered flag
5	Directional signs, printed on lightweight board: right turn, left turn, straight on, toilets, officials only, competitors only, registration, caution – sports event in progress
6	Red Flags: 22 fixed on 4 ft dowels; can be used by officials or as course markers
7	Course marker stakes: 100, each of 45 cm length with yellow flags attached
8	Bunting: 100 yards
9	Portable public address system: radio microphone type, two speakers; state whether indoor or outdoor use when booking

• 2 outdoor horns, stands and cables

• 2 indoor speakers and cables

• 1 tuner/transmitter

• 1 amplifier

• 1 tie-clip microphone

• 1 pocket pack for tie-clip microphone

Power supply: the PA system requires either a mains power supply or a 12 V battery (not supplied) |
10	Portable indoor amplifier with microphone and stand (Laney Linebacker)
11	Megaphone: battery powered with stand and microphone on short cable; charged batteries are supplied
12	Portable team shelters (2) of heavy-duty PVC with an aluminium frame: the three-walled, roofed shelter is approximately 9 ft wide, 5 ft deep and 7 ft high; the kit includes poles 8 ft long; ▷

the shelter is pinned to the ground to secure it in windy conditions; the team shelter is ideal for competitors/officials involved in results, registration or presentation events; it takes around 30 minutes to erect

13 Information/results kiosk of heavy-duty PVC: approximately 4 ft 8 in square and 6 ft 6 in high; the front wall has a small serving ledge and the kiosk can be transported in a small car

14 Awards plinth for presentations: comes in three interlocking sections for first, second and third

15 Seiko electronic stopwatches (2) with printer: facilities include split times and the capacity to record large numbers of times

16 Electronic stopwatches (2) without printer

17 Free-standing, portable flip chart: to advise competitors or post results; comes in carrying case

18 Gas urn with 4.5 kg gas cylinder and regulator to provide hot water for refreshments; a spare gas cylinder is not supplied but is recommended

19 Cold water container: 6 gal with tap and stand; stores water for cold drinks

20 Portable table: 34 in × 24 in, lightweight

21 Twin burner and grill camping stove with 4.5 kg gas cylinder and regulator; a spare gas cylinder is not supplied but is recommended

22 Portable staging: 16 units of staging rostra, each 2 m × 1 m, with various height settings to 1 m; access stairs are provided and the units may be interlocked; can be used indoors or outdoors in dry weather; van transport is required and two persons must carry and load

23 Folding, standard bridge tables (49): only available for card games, indoors

24 Desktop display board: portable, for competitor information or to display results; comes in a carrying case and will fit into a car boot

25 Nimlok photo display boards (looped nylon surface) with stand legs and fittings: for indoor use; supplied in carrying cases; display area is 160 ft^2 when using both sides; boards are 3 ft × 3 ft; can be transported in an average hatchback; use Velcro mounting tape or mounting pads, not Blu-Tack

26 Pinboard art display boards for indoor use: 6 folding panels usable on both sides; unfolded size is approximately 6 ft × 3 ft per panel; metal legs; hooks are supplied (~ 100); transport requires an average to large estate car or hatchback

27 Slide projector with remote facility: 2 carousels, 90 slides

28 Video camera: VHS with rechargeable one-hour and two-hour power packs; borrowers must book any optional extras, e.g. tripod, 3 in colour monitor, telescopic microphone

29 Portable television: colour, 14 in

$\triangleright$

30	Video recorder: VHS with remote controller; tapes not supplied
31	Portable lectern
32	Portable self-contained lectern/amplifier, type MLA 200: state whether batteries or mains power is required
33	Overhead projector
34	Projector stand
35	Film or slide projection screen: height 6½ ft, width 6 ft; fits any car that accommodates rolled length of 6 ft
100	Community sports pack: used on the successful Rural Roadshow and may be borrowed by local community groups; the equipment is stored in holdalls for ease of transportation

- 6 large hoops
- 6 cones
- 1 Unihoc set
- 2 sets of multimarker discs (36 markers per set) incl. goals
- 6 skipping ropes
- assorted beanbags
- 3 sets of bibs in assorted colours
- assorted balls
  - foam
  - rounders
  - airflow
  - tennis
  - football (2)

101	Badminton pack: 24 badminton rackets
102	Cricket pack: 1 set of junior team cricket equipment comprising bats, balls, 2 sets of stumps and holdall; also 6 practice bats and balls
103	Hockey pack: 2 starter packs of sticks, balls, pads, marker cones, bibs and large holdall
104	Football pack: 4 Ramsay lightweight seven-a-side goals, nets and pins; transport requires suitable vehicle and two people
105	Rugby pack: new image rugby starter pack comprising balls, bibs, cones and holdall
106	Squash pack: 24 squash rackets and assorted squash balls; 2 squash training aids
107	Tennis Pack: 24 tennis rackets and 3 sets of short tennis starter packs comprising bats, balls and holdall
108	Short tennis: 2 starter packs of 24 bats and balls; 1 Little Prince ball machine (60-ball capacity) with balls
109	Marker discs: 36 per set

▷

Plymouth Half-Marathon

Key Date Schedule

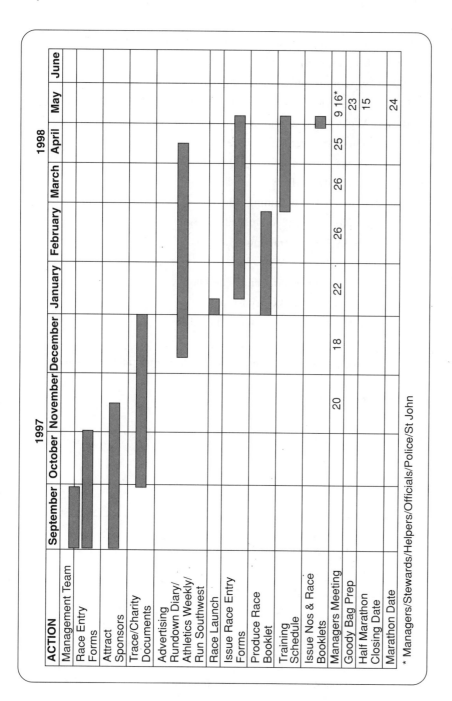

* Managers/Stewards/Helpers/Officials/Police/St John

Press release schedule

06 January 199–	Press release and invitation to sponsors
14 January 199–	Launch, United Services Officers Club, l230
23 January 199–	New course
30 January 199–	Announcement of Schools Competition Fun Run
06 February 199–	Race entry form
13 February 199–	Supporting programme, Plymouth City Council
20 February 199–	Interservice 'Battle Cry' and Plymouth Nuffleld Hospital Feature
27 February 199–	Weeks 1 and 2 training schedule
06 March 199–	School competition update and first timers profile
13 March 199–	Weeks 3 and 4 training schedule
20 March 199–	Corporate challenge
27 March 199–	Weeks 5 and 6 training schedule
03 April 199–	Profile on top Plymouth athlete Bob Wise
10 April 199–	Weeks 7 and 8 training schedule
17 April 199–	
24 April 199–	Weeks 9 and 10 training schedule
01 May 199–	Race update and entry form
08 May 199–	Weeks 11 and 12 training schedule
15 May 199–	
22 May 199–	Race preview and advertising features programme of events, 2–4 pages
24 May 199–	Race update
26 May 199–	Race report, centre spread
27 May 199–	Race results, 4 pages

Project team

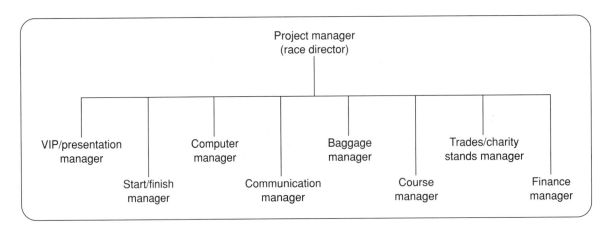

Job descriptions: before/during shows how team size changes

VIP manager

Before event   1
During event   3

● The holder of this post will be responsible for the presentation of the awards.

1. To invite suitable VIPs to the event:
   – Lord Major to start and reception
   – Sponsors
   – City officials from Leisure Services
   – DML directors

2. To ensure that the VIPs are looked after throughout the day.

3. To ensure the VIPs are briefed on their tasks before the event.

4. To ensure that the VIPs are all in the right place at the right time.

5. Be responsible for the layout of the trophies (make a feature).

6. Be responsible for inviting sponsors to make the presentation and making the public and the competitors know who the sponsors are, and what they have contributed.

7. Making the press aware of the timetable.

8. Staffing the presentation area.

9. Be responsible for obtaining signatures of athletes who take perpetual trophies.

Finance manager

Before event   1
During event   2

1. To be responsible for collecting all monies before the event and during the event, from whatever source:
   – race entries
   – fun run
   – race results.

2. To ensure that a balance sheet is prepared (when applicable).

3. To be responsible for the payment of all invoices with the project manager's approval.

4. To be in the appropriate location at the event for collecting monies from the fun run and the race results.

Baggage manager

Before event   1
During event   6

● This post-holder will also liaise with the start/finish, course and trade/charity managers.

1. Ensure that the volunteer groups, such as marshals and water station assistants, are allocated goody bags.

2. To be responsible for the collection of competitors' baggage and the safe keeping and return of such baggage.

3. Ensure that a suitable system is incorporated for the storage and handling of the baggage.

4. Ensure there is an adequate supply of baggage labels.

Course manager

Before event   2
During event   6

● This post-holder will also liaise with the communication manager.
● This post-holder will also be responsible for the provision of water stations.

1. Liaise with staff member SWW before the event and during the event.

2. Liaise with Devon Army Cadets.

3. To be responsible for the marking out and removal of the course direction arrows, mile markers, caution runner and drinks station signs.

4. Ensure that all marshals are in position and fully equipped on the day.

5. Make a provision for the backup vehicle (staffed).

6. Be responsible for disposal of sponges, cups, etc., at the tip.

7. Collect and return all equipment to staff member DML.

8. To be responsible for collection installation and return of road cones.

9. Ensure the distribution of goody bags to marshals and cadets.

Trade/charity stall: roles and responsibilities

Manager
The manager's role is as described on p. 104.

Assistant 1
Assistant 1 should undertake the following tasks in order to assist the trade/charity stall manager in his or her duties:

1. Issuing of contracts and permits to trade/charity stallholders.

2. Point of contact should manager be unavailable.

3. Control access of vehicles on to the Hoe Promenade by ensuring that stallholders and contractors have written permission to enter the arena.

4. Assist in the setting up of equipment and marquees as part of the Hoe layout, including portable fences in the start/finish area.

5. After 9.30 am, to ensure that all vehicles on the Hoe Promenade conform to the conditions of entry. This should be done throughout the whole event.

6. After the race has been started, to assist any of the event managers in the disposition of their duties as required.

7. Once the race has finished, to assist in the dismantling of equipment, marquees, and barriers. To assist in husbandry duties on the Hoe Promenade.

8. To instruct traders to dismantle and clean areas before leaving the promenade.

Assistant 2
See items 3 to 7 above.

Plan of the race

Figure 7.A

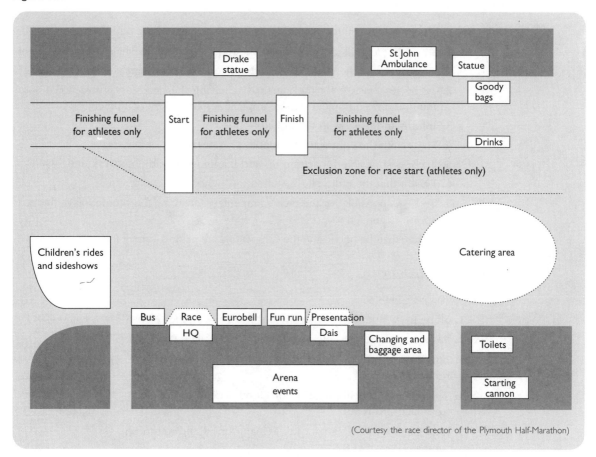

(Courtesy the race director of the Plymouth Half-Marathon)

Trade/charity manager

Before event   1
During event   5

● This post-holder will also liaise with the start/finish and communication managers.
   1. To be responsible for the layout of the trade/charity stand and promenade areas.
   2. Liaising with the start/finish manager, for the race requirement area.
   3. Allocate space to specific organisations and businesses.
   4. Providing advertising, reference tendering.
   5. In conjunction with the project manager, produce the site contract and passes.
   6. Ensure that areas are kept clean (of rubbish and oil) on the day.
   7. Liaise with the finance manager for collecting the site fees.
   8. Ensure that sufficient staff are available for setting up and dismantling equipment.

Communication manager

Before event   1
During event   2

● This post-holder will liaise with the course manager and the trade/charity manager.
● This post-holder will also coordinate the requirement of marshals before the event.
   1. To ensure that the event has an adequate number of marshals.
   2. To be responsible for the marshals receiving the necessary instructions, communications equipment (where applicable) and safety equipment.
   3. Inform and liaise with the police.
   4. Liaise with the contractor to establish a satisfactory PA system.
   5. To be responsible for setting up and manning the radio network and HQ.
   6. Ensure that the radio HQ is staffed throughout the event.
   7. To be responsible for the race commentary, ensuring the promotion of the race sponsors and VIPs.
   8. Ensure that the public and the competitors are made aware of the events timetable.

List of marshals

Start Hoe Promenade

   1. Slope from Hoe, Remain for FR and Return of runners (Posn 54)   1 × M, 1 × P
   2. Pavement to Citadel Entrance, Remain for FR (Return to Hoe)   1 × M
   3. Junc Citadel Rd/Lambhay Hill, Remain for FR and return of runners Posn 55)   1 × M, 1 × P
   4. Top of Lambhay Hill, Remain for FR relocate to top of Hoe Approach (Posn 56)   1 × M
   5. Junc Lambhay Hill/Madeira Rd, Remain for FR and return of runners (Posn 52) **R**   1 × M, 1 × P

6. Junc Madeira Rd/Hoe Rd, Remain for FR and return of
runners (Posn 53) $1 \times M$, $1 \times P$

7. Junc Grand Parade/pier St (Return to Hoe) $1 \times M$, $1 \times P$

8. Junc Grand Parade/Northumberland Tce (Return to Hoe) $1 \times M$

9. Junc Gt Western Rd/west Hoe Rd (Elliot St/Grand Hotel Ope) **R** $1 \times M$, $1 \times P$

10. & **11** Millbay Rd Roundabout (Posn 59 & 60) $2 \times M$, $1 \times P$

12. Junc Millbay Rd/Crescent (Posn 58) $1 \times M$, $1 \times P$

13. Junc Crescent/Princess Way (Posn 57) $1 \times M$, $1 \times P$

14. Junc Notte St/Hoe Approach (Posn 51) $1 \times M$

15. Junc Notte St/Buckwell St (Posn 50) $1 \times M$, $1 \times P$

16. Junc Vauxhall St/Basket Ope (Posn 49) $1 \times M$

17. Junc Vauxhall St/Bretonside (Posn 48) $1 \times M$, $1 \times P$

18. Junc Bretonside/Exeter St (Posn 47) $1 \times M$, $1 \times P$

19. Entrance to Do It All (Posn 46) $1 \times M$

20. & **21** Cattedown Roundabout (Posn 45 & 44) **R** $2 \times M$, $1 \times P$

22. Slip Rd Embankment Rd/Embankment $2 \times M$, $1 \times P$

23. Junc Laira Bridge Rd/Hele Tce $1 \times M$, $1 \times P$

24. Junc Laira Bridge Rd/The Ride $1 \times M$

25. Junc The Ride/Chelson Tip $1 \times M$

26. Gate Entrance to Saltram Park $1 \times M$

27. 2nd Gate, Saltram Park $1 \times M$

28. 3rd Gate, Saltram Park $1 \times M$

29. Crossroads at Saltram House $1 \times M$

30. Stag Lodge Gate **R** $1 \times M$

31. & **32** Stag Lodge Crossing $2 \times M$, $1 \times P$

33. Junc Haye Rd/Elburton Rd $1 \times M$

34. & **35** Elburton Underpass $2 \times M$

36. Stanborough Rd Roundabout $1 \times M$, $1 \times P$

37. Saltram Inn Roundabout (Anchorage) $1 \times M$, $1 \times P$

38. & **39** Billacombe Roundabout $2 \times M$, $1 \times P$

40. Junct Laira Bridge Rd/Finnigans Rd $1 \times M$

41. Maxwell Rd Roundabout $1 \times M$

42. Junc Maxwell Rd/Shapters Way $1 \times M$

43. Junc Macadam Rd/Clovelly Rd $1 \times M$

44. Junc Clovelly Rd/Commercial Rd $1 \times M$, $1 \times P$

45. Crossroads Commercial Rd/Sutton Rd $1 \times M$, $1 \times P$

46. Junc Sutton Rd/Exeter St $1 \times M$

47. Junc Exeter St/Bretonside $1 \times M$

48. Junc Bretonside/Vauxhall St $1 \times M$

49. Junc Vauxhall St/Basket Ope $1 \times M$

50. Junc Notte St/Southside St $1 \times M$, $1 \times P$

51. Junc Vauxhall St/Parade	$1 \times M$
52. Junc Parade/Lambhay Hill/Madeira Rd	$1 \times M, 1 \times P$
53. Junc Madeira Rd/Hoe Rd	$1 \times M, 1 \times P$
54. Base of Slope from Hoe Prom	$1 \times M$
55. Junc Citadel Rd/Lambhay Hill	$1 \times M$
56. Junc Citadel Rd/Hoe Approach	$1 \times M, 1 \times P$
57. Junc Citadel Rd/Lockyer St	$1 \times M, 1 \times P$
58. Junc Citadel Rd/Elliot St	$1 \times M, 1 \times P$
59. Junc Elliot St/Cliff Rd	$1 \times M$
60. Entrance to Hoe	$1 \times M$

Computer manager

Before event   2
During event   4

● This post-holder will also liaise with the start/finish and VIP managers.

1. Responsible for setting up a database of race entries.
2. Providing a race results service.
3. Access to a suitable race results area, in conjunction with the project manager.
4. Liaise with the start/finish manager for the race results.
5. Provide adequate training in conjunction with the start/finish manager.
6. Provide adequate hardware and software.
7. Liaise with the press for pre- and post-race service.

Start/finish manager

Before event   3
During event   12

● The holder of this post will liaise with the VIP and computer managers.

1. Be responsible for setting up the start and finish areas, gantry and funnels in conjunction with the trade/charity stand manager.
2. Ensure that the event has sufficient officials, i.e. referee and timekeepers, and ensure the official rules are complied with.
3. Provide the results of the race to the results area.
4. Provide a results service team.
5. Liaise with the starter, the Royal Artillery and the competitors for the start of each event.
6. Ensure that the race rules are complied with:
   - team colours
   - duplication of numbers
   - non-official race entries

7. Be responsible for providing race results in conjunction with the computer manager and the VIP manager.
8. To be responsible for the allocation of goody bags at the event.

Family tree

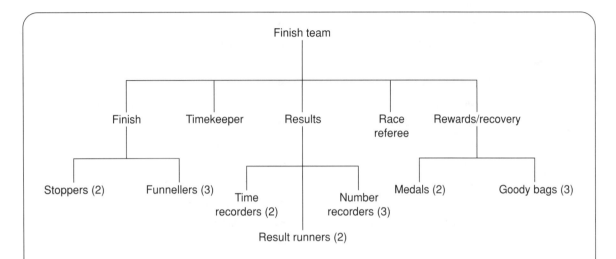

Stopper Stops any runner not having an official number from crossing the finish line.

Funneller Guides the finishing runners into the finishing funnels; ensures that they stay in the correct order and keep moving.

Time recorder Records the times called by the timekeeper as a runner crosses the finish line; passes completed sheets to a results runner.

Number recorder Records a runner's number as the runner leaves the finishing funnel; passes completed sheets to a results runner.

Results runner Collects completed sheets from the time recorder and goes to number recorder when their sheet is complete; takes both sheets to the results manager in the Grand Hotel.

Medal Ensures that all runners who finish the race receive a medal. Required for the fun run and the half-marathon.

Goody bags Ensures that all finishers, and only finishers, receive a goody bag. Required for the fun run and the half-marathon.

This family tree is reproduced courtesy of Nigel Rowe, DML Sports and Social Club

A master event checklist

1. This list has been assembled through experience and research, but no list can be exhaustive.

2. A list needs to be drawn up for each significant event; the master checklist must be adapted to the unique circumstances of the event.

- access times
- accommodation
- accounts
- accreditation
- acoustics
- adhesives
- administration
- admissions
- advertising
- alcohol consumption
- ancillary activities
- ancillary facilities
- animal care
- announcements
- appeals for funds
- appeals for volunteers
- applications (for participants)
- arrival arrangements
- artwork
- audience (to be targeted)
- audiovisual aids
- badges
- banking
- banners
- barriers
- bars
- bookings
- breakout rooms
- budgeting procedures
- cancellations
- car parking
- cash facilities
- cash flow and change
- catering
- ceremonies

- chairs and tables
- changing rooms
- checklists
- Children's Act
- church services
- civic and government receptions
- cleaning
- cloakrooms
- commentators
- committees
- communications
- complaints
- complimentary tickets
- concessions
- contingency plans
- contracts
- copyright
- crèche
- credit facilities
- critical plan document
- customer care
- date
- damage reports
- decoration
- delegate packs
- delivery acceptance
- departure arrangements
- dietary requirements
- diplomacy
- disabled facilities
- dismantling times
- display boards
- displays
- documentation
- drug testing

- electrical services
- elevators
- emergency procedures
- emergency services
- entertainment
- entry arrangements
- equipment
- estimates of income and expenditure
- evaluation (post event)
- event handbook
- exchange facilities
- exhibitions
- facilities at venue
- fax machines
- fencing
- films
- finance
- fire safety
- first aid
- flexibility of response
- float (small change)
- floor plans
- floral decor
- franchise arrangements
- fundraising
- guests
- health and safety
- hearing-impaired provision
- hiring
- hospitality
- hosting
- hotels
- identification
- image
- indemnification documents
- information
- information points
- insurance
- interpreters
- interviews
- invitations
- invoicing
- kiosks
- legal aspects
- liaison officers
- licences (liquor, public entertainment, etc.)
- lifeguards
- lighting
- loading entrances
- local authority
- logo
- lost property
- lost children
- maintenance
- maps
- market research
- master of ceremonies
- medals
- media
- medical provision
- meeting plans
- menus
- message boards
- monitoring
- music
- numbers participating
- nursery (daycare)
- objectives
- offices
- officials
- organisational structure
- passes
- patents
- patronage
- performances
- permits
- personnel
- photocall
- photocopying
- photography

- planning
- policing
- political support
- poster sites
- post-event arrangements
- power supply
- practice facilities
- presentations
- press conference
- press launch
- press room
- prestigious supporters
- printed programme
- printing
- prizes
- programme of the day
- protective clothing
- protocol
- public address system
- publicity
- public relations
- radio
- receipt system
- reception areas
- refreshments
- refuse areas and disposal
- registration
- religious services
- repairs procedures
- research
- safety
- sales
- satellite links
- schedules
- scoreboards
- seating
- secretarial services
- security
- services (plumbing, etc.)
- set-up time

- shops
- sightseeing tours
- signposting
- smoking areas
- souvenirs
- speakers' requirements
- spectator arrangements
- sponsorship
- staffing
- staging
- stationery
- stewards
- stockchecks
- storage
- structures (of organisation)
- subsistence
- Sunday trading law
- support services
- tables
- team liaison
- technical equipment
- technical requirements
- technicians
- telecommunications
- telephones
- temperature
- tickets
- time
- timetable
- toilets
- tourist services
- traders and exhibitors
- traffic control
- training
- translation facilities
- transport
- travel (agents)
- trophies
- TV
- two-way radio

- uniforms
- ushers
- vehicular access
- venues
- VIPs
- visitor facilities

- warm-up
- waste disposal
- weather contingencies
- wheelchair access
- work schedules
- workshops

It would be easy now to fill the rest of this book with a paragraph on each item. This would be less than interesting but, more important, it would not be the most relevant approach, since it is impossible to cover all the issues fully for every event in the field of leisure and tourism.

It is better for individual event organisers to expand on each point for themselves, so the result is appropriate to the event. There is a very simple way to achieve this. Consider each item on the checklist and produce a detailed specification for it. These are the vital questions:

- Is this relevant to our event?
- Is this desirable or essential?
- How much will it cost?
- Can it be afforded?
- Can it be achieved?
- How?
- When?
- By whom?

- Where?
- Where from?
- Where to?
- At what time?
- For whom?
- Who pays cost?
- Can this be obtained for no cost?

Checklists for sport, art and finance

Items from the master checklist should be carried forward into smaller checklists for venue requirements, event timetabling, finance, etc. Here are examples of a financial checklist, an arts event checklist and a sports checklist. By compiling these checklists and allocating the identified tasks to groups or individuals (through detailed job specification documents), a precise and efficient event procedure can be achieved. All that need be added are a timetable and a monitoring system.

Financial checklist

Income

- advertising
- bank interest
- bar sales
- catering sales
- donations
- entry fees
- exhibitors
- franchising and endorsements

- fundraising
- grant aid
- miscellaneous
- other media fees
- patrons
- photograph/video sales
- programme sales
- raffle

- souvenirs
- sponsorship
- tickets
- traders
- TV fees

Expenditure

Costs of

- accountant
- advertising
- bank charges
- banners and bunting
- catering
- cleaning
- consultant fees
- contribution to charity
- copyright fees
- decorations and flowers
- ground rent
- heating
- information technology
- insurance
- legal fees
- lighting
- management fees
- medical fees
- miscellaneous
- PA system
- petty cash
- postage
- press launch and party
- printing (posters, tickets, programmes)
- prizes (engraving)
- repair and maintenance costs
- restoration costs
- staffing
- staff training
- stationery
- telephone
- transport of VIPs

Donations to

- helpers (e.g. selling programmes)
- St John Ambulance and Red Cross

Fees for

- artistic director and producer
- bands
- choirs
- MC and commentator
- secretarial support
- soloists

Hire of

- costumes
- fire extinguishers
- hall or marquee
- Portaloos
- radio
- recording equipment, amp
- scaffolding
- scores
- seating
- uniforms
- venue

An arts event checklist

Facilities for event

- accommodation
- car park
- changing rooms
- cloakrooms
- crèche and childminding
- exhibition areas
- first-aid and medical rooms
- kitchens, food prep
- lavatories
- lost property room
- offices
- official's room
- performers' rooms
- playing area
- poster sites
- press room
- reception areas
- reuse area
- rehearsals
- security rooms
- social, bar and catering areas
- storage
- TV rooms
- warm-up and practice areas

Equipment

- chairs and tables
- communications (e.g. radios)
- decorations
- display boards
- drapes
- fencing and barriers
- flags
- flowers
- generators
- heating
- lighting, TV and emergency
- marquees
- projection equipment
- protective clothing
- public address system
- scoreboards
- screens
- seats
- signs (e.g. no smoking, seat numbers)
- spectator stands
- stage
- uniforms for staff

Staff: full-time, part-time, casual, voluntary

- attendants
- bar staff
- cashiers
- caterers
- cleaners
- cloakroom attendants
- doctor and medical staff
- EGOs
- electricians
- maintenance personnel
- officials
- patrols
- receptionists
- safety lifeguards
- secretaries
- security guards
- standby requirements, training
- stewards
- technicians
- telephonists
- traders and exhibitors
- ushers

Presentation and media

- advertising
- announcers
- ceremonies
- commentators
- dress rehearsals
- entertainment
- films
- interpreters
- interviews
- marketing and PR
- merchandising
- music, performing rights, unions
- photography, photocalls, copyright
- presentation
- press
- prizes and medals
- protocol
- public address
- publicity
- souvenirs
- sponsorship and patronage
- theme, logo and image
- TV and radio
- VIPs

Administration, documentation and finance

- admission, ticket free
- appeals, fundraising, grants
- arrivals and departures
- budget
- cash flow, security and change
- contracts
- copyright
- event handbook
- franchises
- identification and passes
- insurance to cover accidents and cancellations
- invitations
- legal advice
- legal structure
- licensing (extension, entertainment)
- organisation structure
- pricing
- printing
- programmes
- sales
- seating arrangements
- stationery
- stockchecking

Support services

- AA
- bar and catering (public, performers and guests)
- car parking
- changing
- cloakrooms
- emergency procedures
- exhibitions
- hotels
- information
- lost property
- maintenance
- medical
- police
- Red Cross and St John Ambulance
- secretarial
- security
- shops
- shuttle service
- telephone, telex and fax
- transport
- travel agency

This checklist was prepared by prepared by Holohan Architects, Dublin.

A sports event check-off list

SCOTTISH AMATEUR GYMNASTICS ASSOCIATION

An asterisk means delete where necessary

Competition name: _____ Date: _____

Competition check-off list

1 Competition name/title _____

2 Date(s) of competition Day 1 _____ Day 2* _____

3 Venue name and address _____
_____

4 Name of manager/director _____ Tel: _____

5 Times of booking   Day 1   from: _____   to: _____
                             Day 2* from: _____   to: _____

6 Times of warm-up   Day 1   from: _____   to: _____
                             Day 2* from: _____   to: _____

7 Time of competition   Day 1   from: _____   to: _____
                             Day 2* from: _____   to: _____

8 Spectator seating for _____

9 Admission charge   Day 1   adult _____   child _____
                        Day 2*   adult _____   child _____

10 Sponsors name (if any) _____

11 Competition will be   SETS* Day 1*   and   VOLS Day 2

12 Competition organiser:
Name: _____
Address: _____
Tel: _____

Form completed by _____ Date _____

Accommodation

13 Is it required   Yes/No*

14 If Yes in item 13, accommodation will be provided at:
_____
_____
Tel: _____

15 Number of officials:
        (A) Judges: _____   (B) Organisers: _____
        (C) VIPs/SAGA Rep: _____   (D) Others: _____
        (equipment, stewards, etc.)

16 From (A) AM/PM* on _____ to _____
             (B) AM/PM* on _____ to _____
             (C) AM/PM* on _____ to _____
             (D) AM/PM* on _____ to _____

▷

17 Meals will be provided at accommodation   Yes/No*

APPROXIMATE NUMBERS AS PER BOX										
Date										
Breakfast										
Lunch										
Tea										
Dinner										

Judges*
Officials*
VIPs*
Others*

18 Meals will be provided at centre/venue   Yes/No*

APPROXIMATE NUMBERS AS PER BOX										
Date										
Breakfast										
Lunch										
Tea										
Dinner										

Judges*
Officials*
VIPs*
Others*

Reception

19 At venue*   Yes/No*   Start time _____   Number _____
20 At place of accommodation*
                 Yes/No*   Start time _____   Number _____
21 Elsewhere*   Yes/No*   Start time _____   Number _____

Equipment

	Nos	SAGA	Venue	Org	Others
22 Parallel bars					
23 Rings					
24 Horizontal bar					
25 Floor area 12 m × 12 m					
26 Pommel horse					
27 Horse (110, 120 + 135 cm) + fixing chain					
28 Vault run-up (25 m) + board					
29 Reuther boards					
30 Asymmetric bars					
31 Spare set of bars					
32 Beam: senior 120 cm and junior 110 cm					
33 Mats (sufficient for all apparatus to 12 cm min)					
34 Chalk					
35 Chalk stands					
36 Crash					

37 Emery cloth and sandpaper					
38 Tape measures (30 m)					
39 13 A socket points					
40 Extension leads					
41 Stopwatches					
42 Judging slips					
43 FIG judging forms					
44 Score sheets					
45 Competitor numbers					
46 Scorers' tables					
47 Judges' tables					
48 Visual scoreboard(s)					
49 Public address system					
50 Microphone(s) (state whether portable or not)					
51 PA speakers					
52 Cassette player					
53 Cassettes					
54 March-on music					
55 Compulsory exercise music					
56 National anthem on cassette					
57 Flags and poles					
58 Vault numbers (1 to *N*, *N* large)					
59 Competitor seating					
60 Press seating					
61 Scorers' seating					
62 Runners' seating					
63 Announcers' seating					
64 Judges' seating					
65 VIP seating					
66 Typewriter or computer and printer					
67 Duplicating facility and photocopying					
68 Stationery					

Personnel

	Nos	SAGA	Venue	Org	Others
69 Number of neutral judges					
70 Number of British judges					
71 STC					
72 Runners					

73 Scorers					
74 Timekeepers					
75 Announcer					
76 Controller					
77 Stewards Competition					
Seating					
Doors					
VIP					
Tickets					
Car park					
Apparatus					
78 Competitors and participants					
79 Coaches					
80 Typists					
81 Duplicating staff					
82 Scoreboard operators					
83 Music operator					
84 Programme sellers					

Presentations

	Nos	SAGA	Venue	Org	Others
85 To VIPs (local)					
86 To venue and town					
87 To teams (visitors, home teams)					
88 To coaches (visitors)					
89 To head judge					
90 To head of delegation (visitors)					
91 Floral (if any)					
92 (A)					
93 (B)					
94 (C)					
95 Trophies					
96 Medals					

Presenters for

97 _____ as above

Mr/Mrs/Miss   and Mr/Mrs/Miss

Floral presentations, if any	Nos	SAGA	Venue	Org	Others
98					
99					
100					

Press, publicity, radio and TV

	Nos	SAGA	Venue	Org	Others
101 Advance booking service from					
102 Local radio and TV					
103 National radio and TV					
104 Posters					
105 Newspaper advertising Local					
National					
106 Local authority advertising					
107 Press release					

Medical

	Nos	SAGA	Venue	Org	Others
108 Doctor (SAGA/local)					
109 Physiotherapist					
110 Facilities					

Car parking (and passes if necessary)

	Nos	SAGA	Venue	Org	Others
111 Spectators					
112 VIPs and SAGA representatives					
113 Equipment providers					
114 Others					

Printing and ticketing requirements

		SAGA	Venue	Org	Others
115 Meal tickets for	Breakfast				
	Lunch				
	Tea				
	Dinner				

116 Reception invitation for	Venue					
	Accommodation					
	Elsewhere					

117 Entry tickets	Day 1	Day 2				
Competitors						
Judges						
Officials						
Spectators						
Total						

118 Complimentary seat tickets	Day 1	Day 2				
VIPs						
Competitors						
Judges						
Officials						
Others						
Total						

119 Programmes
Number required _____ Cost of programmes _____
Required by _____

Information to

	A,B,C, or D**	SAGA	Venue	Org	Others
120 Team selection					
121 Competition draw details					
122 Competition information					
123 Results					
124 For press					
125					
126					

** A = teams and officials, B = club coaches, C = clubs, D = regions

Miscellaneous and special extra requirements

	Nos	SAGA	Venue	Org	Others
127 Special invitations to					
128 Refreshments other than meals					
129 Insurance					
130					

A fun run checklist

Personnel

- race director
- publicity officer
- athletics club
- runners
- starter
- photographer
- drivers
- licences
- support (political, etc.)
- souvenirs
- post-event services
- press launch
- course manager
- media liaison
- VIPs
- stewards
- timekeeper(s)
- car park attendants
- local authority liaison
- approvals
- media
- work schedule
- press launch
- legal advice
- medical coordinator
- police
- volunteers
- announcer
- technician(s)
- VIP stewards
- permits
- administration
- organisation structure
- support services
- post-event evaluation
- contingency plans

Finance

- controller
- contingencies
- appeals
- patronage
- systems
- estimates
- sponsorship
- traders' stands
- petty cash
- accounts
- sales

Health and safety

- medical cover
- safety certificates
- emergency procedures
- emergency services
- first aid
- stewarding
- radio system
- health and safety legislation
- fire precautions
- traffic control
- ambulances

Warm-up facilities

- crèche
- registration desk
- entertainment
- press facilities

- catering
- changing rooms
- runners' clothing
- PA system
- transport
- telephone
- notices
- waste disposal
- spectator seating
- start/finish areas

- access
- electrical supply
- marquees
- ancillary activities
- exhibitions
- car parking
- hospitality
- lost property
- toilets

Course

- route
- equipment
- policing
- stewarding
- disabled access
- invoicing
- receipt system
- banners
- maps
- direction marking
- cones and tapes
- running surface
- fencing and barriers
- advertising

- cash security
- steward bibs
- course access passes
- signposting
- spectators
- radio communications
- clocks
- mile markers
- fun spot prizes
- banking
- start/finish
- arrangements
- maintenance

Administration

- stationery
- planning documentation
- event timetable
- checklists
- logo

- posters
- entry procedures
- planning meetings
- publicity

Having identified the specific requirements for your run, you will have to

- analyse costs
- identify necessary personnel
- specify the timetable

- construct the plan
- implement the plan

The next stage is to fit this set of requirements into a timescale of action.

Selecting meeting and function rooms

Meeting rooms blocked and assigned for

- general meetings, breakouts, sessions
- food and beverage function space
- committee rooms
- exhibit areas
- opening/closing ceremonies
- office
- hospitality and VIPs
- slide preview space
- registration
- other

Additional meeting rooms held as backup expansion needed
(write them in the space provided below)

Facility personnel on duty

- sales
- event coordinator or site organiser (hours)
- switchboard
- security
- reception
- office support
- housekeeping

Study the physical aspects

- attendee comfort
- speaker focus
- restroom accessibility
- catering accessibility
- exhibitor accessibility
- proximity to public phones, ATMs, vending machines, etc.
- audiovisual feasibility
- traffic flow
- external noise
- access for people with special needs
- vehicle access if required

Focus on the conditions of the rooms

- ventilation
- acoustics (e.g. air walls, waterfall noise)
- obstructions (air wall pockets, ventilation ducts)
- furnishings (e.g. drape classroom tables)
- soundproofing between rooms
- lighting
- access, traffic flow

Figure 7.2 Set-ups for meeting rooms

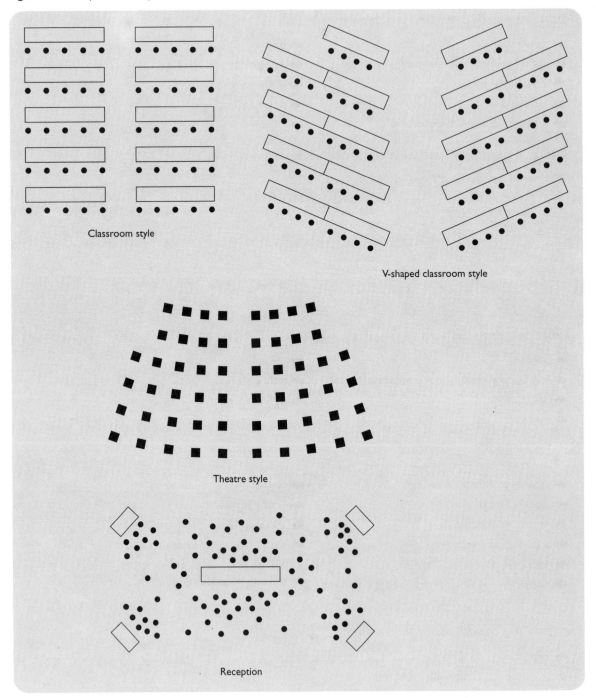

Classroom style

V-shaped classroom style

Theatre style

Reception

Figure 7.2 (Cont'd)

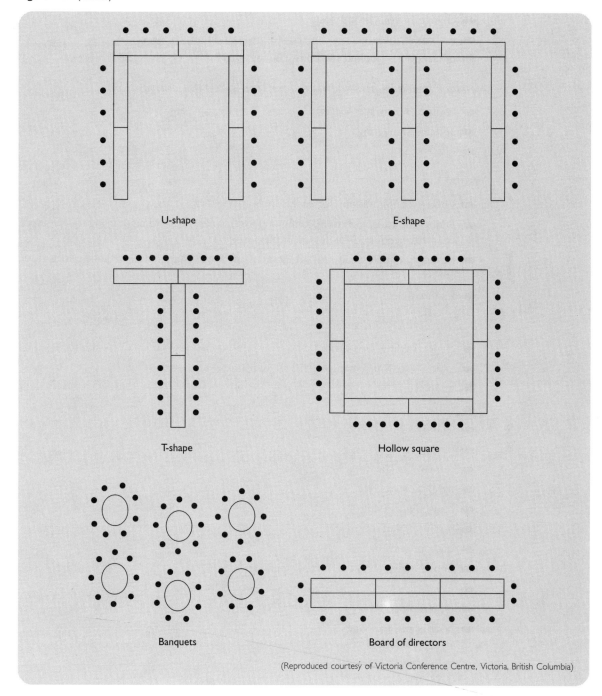

U-shape

E-shape

T-shape

Hollow square

Banquets

Board of directors

(Reproduced courtesy of Victoria Conference Centre, Victoria, British Columbia)

Plan for contingencies

- change in your group size
- availability of larger and smaller rooms, condition, charges
- other groups booked in centre concurrently

Consider space requirements before and after the convention

- equipment storage space
- additional meetings
- office space

Set-ups

- Choose configurations for each function (Fig. 7.2).
- Request mock-ups of room configurations from event coordinator using rooms selected, where required for selection purpose.
- Ensure adequate space for all elements in room (stage, audiovisuals, dance floor, etc.)
- Use rear-view projection.

List equipment requirements

- chairs: folding, boardroom
- tables: 4, 6, 8 ft rectangles, 18, 30 in. rounds
- stage size
- draperies
- lectern
- phone outlets
- runway for theatre
- lighting: spots, etc.
- house lights control
- podium, platform, risers
- microphones
- public address system: mixer, operator
- electricity: AC/DC current, capacities, outlet locations
- extension cords
- boards and messages
  - whiteboards
  - bulletin boards
  - easels
  - flip charts
  - message centre
- audiovisual equipment: total needed versus centre supplied
- supplies
  - notepads
  - pencils

- water and glasses
- flags
- signs
- banners
- piano
- wastebaskets
- table coverings

Inventory VCC supplies. Supplement with outside suppliers if necessary. Determine all charges.

Services and policies

- telephone hook-up
- Signposting
- smoking, non-smoking
- staff management schedules
- beepers, walkie-talkies, house phones
- availability of temporary secretarial service
- rental availability of office equipment: computers, typewriters, etc.
- enquire about all union and centre regulations (e.g. electrical hook-ups)

Charges and booking

Determine if meeting-room charges include the following for your particular event:

- seating
- risers/stages
- special set-ups, repeated setup (in case of errors)
- tables
- head tables

Determine the basis for booking

- 24 hour
- session
- full day

Estimate set-up and teardown times as well as move-in and move-out times. Establish and abide by release dates outlined in the contract.

Draw up tentative and final programmes

- list of function rooms with times and dates
- set-ups for each function
- rooms to be rearranged

Sign contract and sign off any ongoing changes to meeting space.

The above meeting and function checklists are based on a document supplied by Victoria Conference Centre, Victoria, British Columbia.

Conference checklists

Success in conference and function promotion may be impaired by failing to anticipate customer needs or neglecting to provide services which have been specifically asked for. These lists may help to jog your memory.

Reservation checklist

1. Number attending.
2. Past information on rooms required: number and type.
3. Pattern of arrivals and departures.
4. Accommodation required: number of rooms and rates.
5. Complimentary accommodation: number of rooms, type and use.
6. Hospitality suites for official use of the buying organisation: number, type and rate.
7. Procedure for reservations: reserved by the organisation or by the individual; payment made by organisation, by individual or complimentary.
8. Accommodation unassigned to .... released by .... date.
9. Procedure for keeping conference official and hotel representative informed on number of reservations, cancellations, etc.

Meeting-rooms reservation checklist

1. Rooms reserved when conference or function booked: number, type and charges.
2. Assignment of specific rooms for functions.
3. Policy for use of meeting rooms during conference or function and outside meeting hours of conference or function.
4. Check condition of meeting rooms: cleanliness, furnishings, ventilation, lighting and acoustics.
5. Check time schedules: times of meetings, location, notices and other signs about meetings.
6. Facilities, equipment and services: check sources both internal and external. Check for ordering and delivery.
7. Detailed instructions for meeting rooms given and checked.
8. Final check of all room arrangements.

Meeting-rooms checklist

1. Space available: floor plan, access area, obstructions, floor load, general appearance, ventilation, lighting, entrances and exits, access to electrical and other services, limitations of these services.
2. Access to space for exhibition: street, doorways, corridors, lifts and their limitations.
3. Rental charge for space: rate. Coverage: area, facilities and equipment.
4. Floor plan.

5. Exhibition stands: location, layout, height and floor load limits.

6. Facilities, equipment and services: check sources, availability and charges.

7. Utilities and limitation: check lighting, power points, etc.

8. Stand decorations: signs, delivery schedules and labour.

9. Exhibit times: space available. Setting-up, exhibiting and dismantling.

10. Admission policy.

11. Security arrangements, insurance, fire and licence requirements.

12. Provision of detailed information for exhibitors.

Detailed checklist of facilities, equipment and services required

1. The room: layout, suitability and seating capacity.

2. Layout: type of function, capacity of room, seating arrangements, tables, chairs, spacing and general layout, accessibility to tables and chairs.

3. Condition of room: cleanliness, furnishings, ventilation, lighting, table coverings, pads, pencils, ashtrays, matches, water glasses for speakers and water.

4. Speaker's table: location, elevation, number of seats, cover, place cards, gavel and reference material.

5. Rostrum.

6. Signal systems.

7. Public address system: microphones and volume control.

8. Lights: regular, sport, adequacy and controls.

9. Blackboards, charts, display stand, chalk dusters and location of supply table.

10. Projection equipment: overhead projector, projector screen, operator, location of machine and screen, films and slides. Suitability of machine for room Plug sizes and points. Table, stand, extension wiring and house lights control.

11. Projection operator, time schedule for receipt and return of materials. Source of materials and equipment.

12. CHECK THE ABOVE BEFORE THE CONFERENCE REQUIRES THE FACILITIES.

13. Reference materials for speakers and for the audience.

14. Miscellaneous: location of telephones, cloakroom facilities and parking facilities. Check they are clearly signposted.

15. Photographer: instructions to be given when required, time to take pictures, how pictures sales have to be handled and equipment set up in advance.

16. Reporting: speeches to be reported. Release cleared. Instructions to be given on type of report, number of copies and time when report will be required.

17. Service of morning coffee, afternoon tea, luncheon and dinner.

18. Conference and other signs and their location.

19. Decoration: flowers, plants, flags and banners.

20. Entertainment: requirements known? Dressing rooms and other facilities required.

21. Publicity: press conference, speakers, press releases and arrangements for press.

22. Final programme information check. Agree it with organisers.

Checklist for food and beverage function

1. Type of function: business, social, dance, part of conference, dinner dance, wedding, funeral or other.
2. Rooms required: type and size, floor plan, seating capacity, decor, lighting, acoustics, ventilation, maintenance and housekeeping charges.
3. Costs: room, food, drink, services, gratuities, entertainment and decorations.
4. House rules, licences and other controls.
5. Time schedules: room preparation, doors open, top-table guests, assembly and entry, cocktails, aperitif, food service, tables cleared, music, speakers and dancing.
6. Room preparation: number expected, scale plan, type of function, furniture required, stage or platform, access aisles, lighting required, decorations, public address system, acoustics, ventilation, other facilities and equipment.
7. Table service or buffet arrangements: number attending, table size, shape, seating capacity, chairs and aisles.
8. Top-table guests assembly: assembly room, bar service, time of assembly, host or hostess, line-up arrangements for seating and usher.
9. Top table: location, size, seating, chairs, number, place cards, decorations, special drinks, cigars and cigarettes, accounting record of number served and special service.
10. Lectern: check if required.
11. Menus: charges for each meal. Cover charges.
12. Type of service required.
13. Best estimate, guarantee of covers needed: deadline day.
14. Beverages function room service: type, ordering time, charges, glasses, return of unused beverages, unopened bottles and opened bottles.
15. Materials for distribution: table identification cards, table notices, place cards, menus, programmes and agenda.
16. Identification badges and methods of admission.
17. Instruction for special admission problems.
18. Facilities, equipment and services: availability and sources.
19. Lighting, public address system and decoration: check they are in order.
20. Special services: cloakrooms, transport, parking and telephones.
21. Ticket service: attendants.
22. Reporters, recorders, photographers and projection equipment.
23. Entertainment requirements.
24. Signs and publicity.

This section is included courtesy of David Leslie, Glasgow Caledonian University.

Specimen job remits

BOARD OF DIRECTORS (EXECUTIVE COMMITTEE)

General description

The board of directors is legally and morally responsible for the overall governance of the event.

Activities and tasks

- Develop a strategic plan with vision, goals and outcomes.
- Establish appropriate beliefs, mission by-laws of the event.
- Establish policies and guidelines to describe how the board will govern and organise its work, e.g. organisational flow chart, hiring policies, leadership style and image.
- Hire and recruit the event manager.
- Define the roles, responsibilities and accountabilities of the event manager.
- Approve overall plans, strategies and budgets.
- Oversee the recruitment, selection and training of the divisional managers.
- Monitor financial and human resources, e.g. budget, revenues and expenditures, staff and volunteers.

Line of authority

The board of directors assumes the ultimate authority and accountability for all aspects of the event.

EVENT MANAGER

General description

The event manager is responsible for the overall management and administration of the event.

Activities and tasks

- Develop an operational plan from the strategic plan prepared by the board of directors.
- Prepare financial statements and a budget for approval.
- Prepare an event manual with guiding principles, policies and procedures, roles and responsibilities, etc.
- Forecast problems and solutions.
- Hire and recruit divisional managers and define their roles, responsibilities and authorities.
- Facilitate communication among divisions.

- Provide ongoing feedback and evaluation to the divisional managers.
- Provide support needed by the divisional managers to function effectively.
- Prepare documentation and reports for board meetings and approvals.

Line of authority

The event manager reports directly to the board of directors. The executive committee of the board of directors provides the event manager with advice and support on the day-to-day operations of the event.

ADMINISTRATION MANAGER

General description

The administration manager is responsible for all personnel procedures and activities contained in the administration division. These include

- bids
- personnel
- finance
- legal
- insurance
- organisational structure
- evaluation and wrap-up

Activities and tasks

- Recruit personnel to coordinate each administration area.
- Define clearly the roles, responsibilities and authority of each coordinator and committee.
- Assist the coordinators in the overall planning for each area.
- Coordinate personnel, policies and procedures, and activities within the administration division.
- Provide the necessary support for coordinators and committees to complete the assigned tasks and responsibilities.
- Facilitate communication among all administration coordinators and among appropriate personnel from other divisions.
- Communicate with other divisional managers.
- Supervise personnel and approve policies.
- Evaluate the administration division and make recommendations to the event manager.

Line of authority

The administration manager reports directly to the event manager.

VOLUNTEER COORDINATOR

General

The volunteer coordinator is responsible for the coordination of all the volunteers needed for the event.

Duties

- Identify what personnel are needed and what skills they require.
- Devise and implement a plan for recruiting required volunteers.
- Develop job descriptions for every post.
- Allocate recruits to appropriate jobs, having defined the tasks and lines of authority.
- Plan and progress procedures for volunteer organisation and operation, e.g. illness, meal allowance, overtime.
- Maintain and update information on necessary resources.
- Retain a small pool of volunteers available on short notice.
- Devise a detailed programme for all volunteers.
- Arrange additional training needed for volunteers to perform their specific job functions.
- Develop an accreditation system.
- Evaluate operations and provide recommendations to the overall event manager.

Reporting to

Personnel director

Operating with

Volunteers committee covering necessary specialist areas.

SPONSORSHIP COORDINATOR

General

The sponsorship coordinator is responsible for obtaining relevant sponsorship for the event and for developing good relationships with the sponsor(s).

Duties

- Define and describe the details of the organisation and the events.
- Liaise with other coordinators and directors to determine possible sponsorship opportunities.

▷

- Determine exactly what you have to offer in exchange for what the sponsor is giving.
- Develop plans and presentations to illustrate the value of the sponsor.
- Negotiate the sponsorship deal and the relationship with the sponsor.
- Liaise with the protocol and hospitality coordinators to ensure the sponsor is treated well.
- Liaise with PR coordinators to ensure maximum publicity coverage is obtained for all sponsors.
- Evaluate sponsorship operations and prepare recommendations for the over-all event manager.

Reporting to

Marketing director

Operating with

A small group of experts supports the sponsorship coordinator in liaison with the PR committee.

The job remits for the board of directors, the event manager and the administration man-ager are reproduced courtesy of David Wilkinson, Wilkinson GP.

Some organisational structures

Figure 7.B

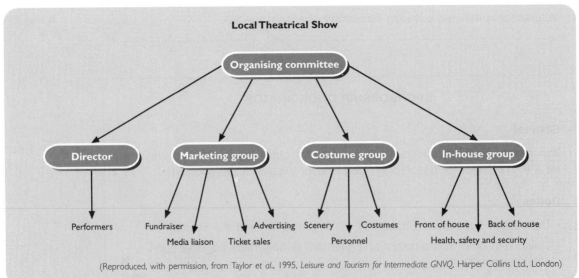

(Reproduced, with permission, from Taylor et al., 1995, *Leisure and Tourism for Intermediate GNVQ*, Harper Collins Ltd., London)

Figure 7.C

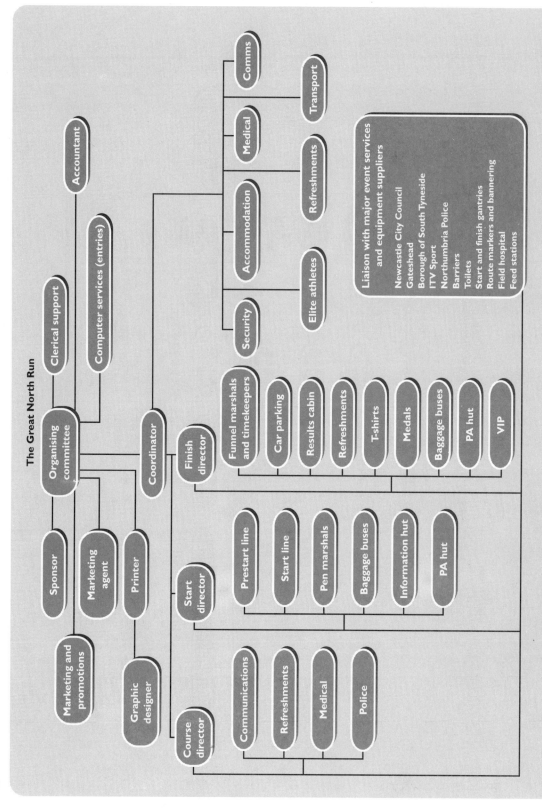

The Great North Run

(Courtesy Nigel Gough and Nova International)

Figure 7.D

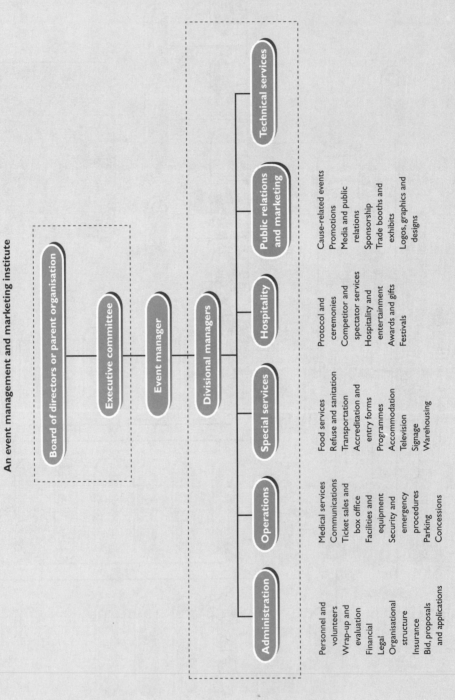

An event management and marketing institute

Board of directors or parent organisation

Executive committee

Event manager

Divisional managers

| Administration | Operations | Special services | Hospitality | Public relations and marketing | Technical services |

Personnel and
volunteers
Wrap-up and
evaluation
Financial
Legal
Organisational
structure
Insurance
Bid, proposals
and applications

Medical services
Communications
Ticket sales and
box office
Facilities and
equipment
Security and
emergency
procedures
Parking
Concessions

Food services
Refuse and sanitation
Transportation
Accreditation and
entry forms
Programmes
Accommodation
Television
Signage
Warehousing

Protocol and
ceremonies
Competitor and
spectator services
Hospitality and
entertainment
Awards and gifts
Festivals

Cause-related events
Promotions
Media and public
relations
Sponsorship
Trade booths and
exhibits
Logos, graphics and
designs

(Courtesy David Wilkinson, Wilkinson Group, Ontario)

Figure 7.E

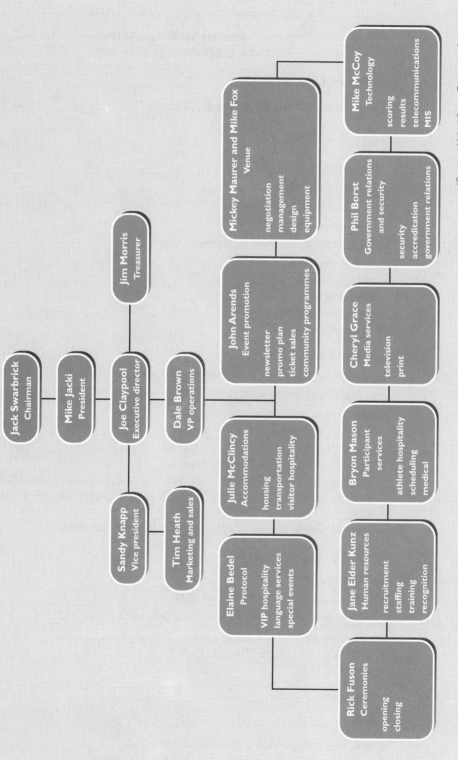

World Gymnastics Championships 1991

Jack Swarbrick
Chairman

Mike Jacki
President

Sandy Knapp
Vice president

Joe Claypool
Executive director

Jim Morris
Treasurer

Tim Heath
Marketing and sales

Dale Brown
VP operations

Elaine Bedel
Protocol

VIP hospitality
language services
special events

Julie McClincy
Accommodations

housing
transportation
visitor hospitality

John Arends
Event promotion

newsletter
promo plan
ticket sales
community programmes

Mickey Maurer and Mike Fox
Venue

negotiation
management
design
equipment

Rick Fuson
Ceremonies

opening
closing

Jane Elder Kunz
Human resources

recruitment
staffing
training
recognition

Bryon Mason
Participant services

athlete hospitality
scheduling
medical

Cheryl Grace
Media services

television
print

Phil Borst
Government relations and security

security
accreditation
government relations

Mike McCoy
Technology

scoring
results
telecommunications
MIS

(Courtesy United States Gymnastics Federation)

A *planning schedule*

NORTH WEST WATER
CYCLE SUNDAY 11 MAY 1997

Areas of responsibility

Cycling project for the North West (CP)

- budget
- route
- administration of entries
- mailouts to participants
- ordering of event equipment
- arranging key meetings
- organisation of activities in Heaton Park
- distribution of posters:
  - cycling clubs
  - bike shops
  - local businesses
  - sites on route

Healthstart Limited (HS)

- all design and printing (all proofs to CP and NWW)
- promotion and public relations
- public liability insurance
- distribution of posters
  - North West Water
  - Local authorities (and sports centres)
  - Manchester, Bury and Bolton city centre outlets (via Arts About Manchester)
  - Mailing list of 1300 entrants to 1996 HealthStart Liverpool–Chester Bike Ride
  - NHS organisations in the North West (and all hospitals)

North West Water (NWW)

- sponsorship
- distribution of posters, sites and staff
- competition card to be designed and printed
- support on day
  - mobile visitor centre, Heaton Park
  - water at finish

Programme

January

Agreed sponsorship with North West Water
HS Press release issued to cycling press and magazines

February

HS	Feb 7: final artwork agreed for entry forms and posters
HS	Feb 14/7: entry forms and posters delivered to Healthstart Ltd and Cycling Project
CP/HS	Feb 17–21: distribution of posters (see responsibilities) North West Water Local authorities (and sports centres) Manchester, Bury and Bolton city centre outlets (via Arts About Manchester) Mailing list of 1300 entrants to 1996 HealthStart Liverpool–Chester Bike Ride NHS organisations in the North West (and all hospitals) Cycling clubs Bike shops Local businesses Sites on route
HS	Feb 17–21: press releases to media in Greater Manchester and East Lancashire
NWW	Feb 28: first payment of sponsorship to Cycling Project by North West Water
CP	TBA: site meeting in Heaton Park
CP	TBA: site meeting at halfway point (Clough Head Information Centre)
CP	TBA: route to be finalised and sites for stewards and AA signage agreed
HS	Training programme to be written and printed
HS	'Welcome card' to be written and printed
NWW	Competition card to be agreed and printed (by North West Water)
HS	Charity sponsorship form to be agreed and printed
HS	T-shirt design to be agreed
CP	Participant numbers to be ordered
CP	Computer system set-up to handle entries
HS	Confirm photographer for the event

February/March

CP	Equipment from event services and other suppliers (gantry, bannering, PA, marquee with tables and chairs, chemical toilets, safety pins, stewards' reflective jackets and bibs, route signage, two-way radios, mobile telephones, minibuses, barriers and tape) to be ordered
CP/HS	Key personnel to be contacted and secured for the event (route stewards, car parking stewards, Raynet communications, first aid, commentator, vehicle drivers, bike mechanics)
ALL	Support services on route to be agreed

▷

March

HS	Mar 3–17: T-shirts to be printed; 'what happens on the day' letter to be agreed and printed
CP	Mar 24–27: First mailout to entrants (large envelopes required); this will include letter explaining what happens on the day
	welcome card
	training programme
	charity sponsorship form
	event number
	T-shirt
	any other information required, e.g. on charities
	safety pins
CP	Mar 26: full meeting of all key parties (2 pm, Cycling Project)
CP	Preparation of activities in Heaton Park
HS	Agree design of finishing certificates
HS	Press releases as entries start to come in
HS/NWW	TBA: Senior figure from North West Water for photocall
NWW	Mar 30: second and final payment of sponsorship to Cycling Project by North West Water

April

CP	Second and third mailouts to entrants as and when necessary
HS	Finishing certificates to be printed
CP/NWW	Order refreshments for finish, minimum water
HS	Press releases

May

ALL	Briefing to all key personnel
CP/HS	May 6–9: produce final information required on day
	computer printouts (alphabetical and numerical) briefing for media and commentators ensure all equipment is available
	pens, pins, numbers T-shirts, entry forms welcome cards (for entrants) certificates and bottled water (for finishers)
CP	May 10: delivery of equipment to Heaton Park if necessary
ALL	**Event day**
HS	Press releases
CP/HS	Thankyou letters

June

ALL	Evaluation and debrief meetings
CP	Preparation of labels for mailout in 1998

This section has been reproduced courtesy of Robin Ireland, Healthstart Limited.

An action agenda

1 Minutes of last meeting

2 Matters arising

3 Recap on previous days' activities
   (a) Problems encountered
   (b) Achievements
   (c) Remedial action to be taken

4 Goals for the next period
   (a) Are they still achievable?
   (b) Problems envisaged at this stage

5 Prioritising of activities
   (a) What is strictly necessary to achieve targets?
   (b) What is no longer appropriate?

6 Allocation of tasks

7 Drawing up of work schedules

This is very much an action agenda; it may help to get action towards a purpose. Two additions would be worthwhile:

- a time limit on each item
- an 'action by' section

The meeting should produce a checklist minute, stating what was agreed, what is to be done, by whom and when.

Sheffield's Event Rider

(By permission of Martin Morton, Sheffield City Council)

SHEFFIELD EVENTS UNIT EVENT RIDER

Event	
Date(s)	
Venue	
Promoter	
Event contacts	
Ticket sales	

▷

Ticket prices	
Number of spectators	
Number of competitors and officials	
Programme of games	
Doors open to public	
Areas used	
Venue set-up	
Venue dismantle	
Accreditation details	
Car park	
Equipment	
Television	

▷

Media	
Lighting requirements	

Catering
  Public
 	
  Guests
 	
  Officials
 	
  Volunteers	

Hospitality	
Merchandising	

Technical support
  Domestic arrangement
 	
  Security
 	
  Electrical/mechanical
 	
  Heating/ventilation
 	
  Other	

Emergency services
  First aid
 	
  SYMAPS
 	
  Licensing	

Police Fire officer	
Accommodation requirements	
Transport requirements	
Communications	
Stewarding	
Abbreviation	

CIRCULATION

Writing press releases

A press release sets out to tell the main point of its subject matter as succinctly as possible. A useful mnemonic is WHAT. It gives the sequence for a typical press release:

What has happened   The introduction must tell the story in a nutshell
How it happened   The explanation should follow immediately
Amplify: Each point in turn
Tie   Tie up all loose ends

Layout

- Make each sentence a paragraph; this makes it easier for the editor.
- Use double spacing and wide margins.
- Type on one side only.
- Ensure it is dated.
- Don't run sentences from one page to the next.
- If more than one page long, type 'MORE' at the bottom of the page.
- At end of the text, type ENDS.
- Include relevant contact names, addresses, telephone and fax numbers at the end.
- Make sure it is submitted before the appropriate press deadline.

Points

- Hit them with a headline!
- Be clear, concise and factual; never ramble.
- Keep the first sentence to a maximum of 20 words.
- It may be useful to include notes to the editor (background information to help expand on items in the article).
- Any accompanying photographs should be clearly captioned on the back. If possible, supply both monochrome and colour. Order extra copies in case of requests.
- Don't use clichés or jargon.
- Check all facts in the text.
- Try to keep the press release below $2\frac{1}{2}$ pages.
- Anticipate any questions arising from the press release, so that answers may be given immediately. Make sure that relevant staff know about its issue.
- If an embargo is required, make sure it is clearly shown at the top and bottom of each page.
- Remember, if placing an advertisement, some publications may be keener to take a press release as well.
- Check you've answered these questions:
  - Who?   – Why?
  - What?   – How?
  - Where?   – Is it interesting?
  - When?

A sample press release

SCOTTISH AMATEUR GYMNASTICS ASSOCIATION

8b Melville Street, Falkirk FK1 1HZ   Tel: 01324 612308

PRESS RELEASE

<u>WORLD'S BEST IN SCOTLAND</u>

For the first time ever, a touring Soviet Gymnastics Team will give performance in Scotland.

A superb line-up of international gymnasts will appear, amongst them Soviet, World and Olympic Champions, showing all aspects of the sport – Men's and Women's Artistic, Rhythmic and Sports Acrobatics.

Prominent amongst the performers will be the legendary Natalia Yurchenco who revolutionised women's vaulting with the incredible 'back flip' approach to the horse. Also on show will be some of the new Soviet Gymnasts, including the amazing Denis Fyodorov (USSR Champion and in 1991 winner of the prestigious French Cup, and several past World Champions).

The support of both Glasgow Sports Promotion Council and the City of Aberdeen District Council has been crucial to staging these enthralling performances in Glasgow and Aberdeen.

–MORE–

This will be a superb opportunity for the thousands of Scots gymnasts and other interested children and adults to witness at close hand the daring and exciting skills performed.

A superb show is in prospect:

Monday 24 February:	Kelvin Hall, Glasgow	7.00 pm to 9.00 pm
Tuesday 25 February:	Beach Leisure Centre, Aberdeen	7.30 pm to 9.30 pm

Tickets for the two spectaculars are available from the venues and further information from the Scottish Gymnastics Office:

SAGA
8b Melville Street
Falkirk
FK1 1HZ

Tel: 01324 612308
Fax: 01324 612309

–ENDS–

Venue preparation

The huge increase in popular ballet and opera during the 1980s brought with it a new phenomenon to the large-scale temporary theatre. This can involve the construction over a period of 3–7 days of a 3000–5000 seat auditorium, a stage with flying facilities and dressing-room or office accommodation for up to 400 people. The high cost of touring large international productions means that larger audiences than those which can be accommodated in traditional theatres need to be provided for in order to generate the box office revenue required for financial viability. Large, high spaces are required to cater for the size of the audience and scale of scenery from companies such as the Bolshoi or Kirov. The only such spaces conveniently located within large cities are multipurpose exhibition halls or sports arenas.

Although some modern exhibition venues were designed with the staging of pop concerts as part of the brief, the idea of producing full-scale opera or ballet was never envisaged. Large auditoria with open stages in traditional theatres are recognised as demanding exacting safety standards from designers and operators alike, but their construction and operation on a *temporary basis* adds an additional dimension to the potential risks.

Fire separation

A temporary large-scale theatre usually requires the construction of three principal areas: a tiered seating area, a stage with flying facilities and dressing-room accommodation. Because of the noise factor, dressing rooms are usually located in an ancillary hall, thereby providing fire separation from the auditorium. It is not possible, however, to provide temporary fire separation between the stage and the auditorium. Where productions (e.g. *Carmen* at Earls Court) are originated in Britain, one can be confident that the scenery will meet the standards for 'open stages'. However, some productions touring from overseas, especially from Eastern bloc countries, have scenery which is both old and without any fire-resisting qualities.

Smoke control

In determining the relative suitability of venues, a study of the smoke extraction system and smoke reservoirs is essential before any layout plans are prepared. Without such a study, the tiered seating could easily be built up within the potential smoke layer. Smoke screens may need to be installed to increase reservoir capacity or channel smoke in particular directions, depending on the layout. As most of these promotions occur during the summer, to appeal to tourists, roof lights and vents are often blacked. Careful attention is required to ensure the performance of the smoke extraction system is not interfered with.

Access

To reduce the problems which can arise when 5000 people arrive at a venue within a space of an hour, needing easy access to and from catering and toilet facilities during the intervals, and safe egress in the event of an emergency, a number of separate access routes should be provided. The number will depend on the size of the audience. Ticket holders should be directed to designated car parks near each entrance, so they can gain access through doors close to where they are sitting. Each access route should have sufficient toilet and catering facilities to cope with the number using the entrance. The traditional crush bar is not desirable in large temporary venues. Fortunately, the desire to maximise refreshment sales means that adequate space is often provided. However, the space required is sometimes underestimated, and concentration of facilities in one area is common, creating serious congestion and contraflow problems in circulation routes. Where temporary catering areas are built, a close watch has to be kept to avoid the introduction of bottled gas or any form of naked flame. The storage and regular removal of refuse must also be monitored carefully to avoid the accumulation of refuse bags at exits.

Location of exits

For both acoustic and aesthetic reasons, the seating area is often surrounded with heavy drapes to form a sense of enclosure. This can have the effect of blocking all final exits from direct sight of the audience, which can make patrons uneasy. It is advisable that all vomitories, aisles, exit routes and doors are staffed by stewards, who can direct the audience in the event of an emergency and open the exit doors. A carefully phrased announcement highlighting the location of the exits, reinforced by ushers pointing to the relevant routes (as per airline procedures) can help both the speed and even distribution of the audience exiting.

Signage

Clear, unambiguous, well-lit signage is essential in temporary venues. If people have to stop to study a sign, in order to determine which way to go, delays and congestion will result. A full schedule of signage should be prepared by the designer, together with the front of house manager and tour manager, and their positions carefully considered and agreed in plenty of time to allow for alterations on site.

Certification

The insistence of each contractor and supplier providing certification by an approved body of the various installations and equipment reduces the likelihood of problems arising. In terms of construction, this means that any proposals must be certified by a structural engineer to the effect that the seating, stage, etc., have been designed to meet the various British Standards and codes of practice. Certification of the as-built structure is also essential.

Be very careful when a supplier says, 'I have a fire cert.' The certificate may simply confirm that the product is entirely inappropriate for the particular use proposed. The supplier, nonetheless, will be fully confident of the product's suitability because they have 'a cert' which they simply do not understand; carpet suppliers to the exhibition industry often fall into this category. Promises from the technical director of a touring company of certificates for the scenery should be investigated well before any decisions are made. On translation you may find that the certificate comes from the workshop of the theatre and is signed by the chief carpenter!

Efforts to treat scenery when on site have in the past resulted in accusations that state works of art are being vandalised. The consequences of scenery not meeting agreed standards should be clearly explained from the outset to visiting companies. A showdown twenty-four hours before the tour opens is not in anybody's interest.

Staffing

It has often been assumed that by employing a front of house (FOH) manager and his or her staff from a local theatre, no problems will occur on the night. Nothing could be further from the truth. Most FOH managers come as close to having nervous breakdowns during the forty-eight hours before opening night at a temporary theatre than they will ever have in their lives.

Changes in seating layouts, due to last-minute demands for larger lighting or sound control positions, or unforeseen construction difficulties with the seating structure, can mean that on occasions up to 300 people need to be reseated on the night. No matter how clear a seating plan is produced, staff will be disorientated in a new venue. It is essential that every member of the FOH staff walks the entire auditorium on a number of occasions, through every aisle and stair. Particular care must be taken when the traditional Saturday matinée takes place with up to 5000 overexcited children. It is advisable that each group leader or teacher is instructed on what to do in the event of an emergency.

Construction

The standard of construction and finishes varies hugely in temporary theatres, as does the competence of the contractors themselves. Specialist contractors provide seating, stage and rigging equipment. But occasionally, for financial or political reasons, the local scaffolding contractor is employed, with potentially disastrous consequences. The standards of installed platforms or stairs for a building site or a sporting event are unacceptable in a theatre. The number of trip hazards and dangerous projections can be enormous unless the types of fixings and construction detailing are gone through thoroughly with each contractor.

Programme

Critical path analyses are carried out on all large building projects. In normal circumstances the programme is divided into weekly units, but in temporary theatre construction it is divided into hours. It is vital that *all* contractors are present at planning meetings to discuss cooperation with the show production team. Each contractor should clearly explain where they will be working, when, with what equipment, what trucks will arrive and when they will need to access the venue for deliveries. The production team need to explain when rehearsals or lighting and sound checks are scheduled, and what work may continue during those times. An unscheduled blackout for focusing can be more than just a surprise for a rigger climbing a roof truss to fix some draping!

Seating

When preparing detailed seating plans, it is important to understand the limitations of the various assembly systems. Some promoters rely on seating plans drawn up by seating contractors whose objective is to fit in the most seats. Experience has shown that these layouts have not been prepared with the capacity of each aisle as a consideration and it is not uncommon for a series of aisles to converge on a cross gangway of equal width to each aisle connected with it.

Vomitories are often constructed with the width of a seatway (i.e. 700–760) as a landing on top. The handrails and stairs, because they are installed within the structure of the seating grid, are often reduced to 1200 wide, whereas 14,000 is indicated on drawings. The lighting of the aisles and the positioning of illuminated exit signs need careful consideration.

Stage and rigging

Until recently, temporary theatres relied on truss systems (or space frames) suspended from the roof of a hall to support lighting grids and various tab tracks. Backdrops were usually dropped to the floor during scene changes. But the production of the Bolshoi Opera at the Scottish Exhibition & Conference Centre in 1990 broke new ground. A complete flying system, incorporating forty-two single-purchase counterweighted lines were installed for seven shows. Because of the enormous weights of the clothes and scenery being flown, the entire system had to be ground supported, using motorway shoring.

Where ground support is not proposed, the location of hanging points for a grid has to be carefully studied. Old exhibition halls with wrought-iron trusses present particular difficulties in trying to determine safe working loads. Lighting bridges are also hung from the roof structure on occasions. A last-minute decision by the lighting designer of the Bolshoi Opera in Glasgow last year, two days before the opening night, meant that an additional 5 tons of equipment needed to be supported on the temporary lighting bridge.

Lighting and special effects

The connected electrical load for large-scale productions is usually 500 to 600 A per phase, although the live load rarely exceeds 500 A per phase. Because of the temporary nature of the installation, literally miles of cable can be installed. Unless detailed drawings of cable runs are produced at an early stage, cables will end up running across aisles and circulation routes. To exacerbate the problem, these cables are often covered with carpet, which simply conceals the hazard.

A thorough check of lighting and special effects equipment should be made when the equipment is delivered on site. If a tour has originated from an Eastern bloc country, the likelihood is that the equipment will be old, not earthed and probably 120 V (without transformers). A dry ice machine produced by one company recently consisted of an 'autoclave unit' (without safety values) producing high-pressure steam, which was in turn blown across a basket of ammonia. The two blond operators were easily recognisable from the rest of the company!

Project management

The project director for the procurement of a temporary theatre needs a broad range of skills and experience in theatre design, budgeting, contract programming, production requirements, theatre management. Safety and financial controls. This combination of technical, operational and financial skills is essential where £1.7 million is spent on seven shows, during the Bolshoi's visit to Glasgow; or £1 million is spent on a single night, the 1988 Eurovision Song Contest.

The intense time pressure under which temporary facilities have to be built can only increase the safety risks that are normally associated with theatres. Extreme diligence is required throughout the planning and construction to ensure these major and spectacular productions are remembered for the right reasons.

This section was prepared by Gar Holohan, architect and leisure consultant.

A simple timetable for local events

At least one month in advance

1. Obtain the necessary venue and facilities.
2. Confirm booking (in writing).
3. Prepare event outline.
4. Obtain the support of necessary personnel.
5. Send information about the event to everyone involved:
   – entry details
   – arrangements for participants
   – transport and accommodation
6. Ensure that necessary permits or licences have been obtained.
7. Make arrangements to obtain all necessary specialist equipment.
8. Plan to obtain all necessary presentation materials, e.g. certificates and medals.

At least two weeks before

1. Advise relevant media of the event arrangements.
2. Arrange for necessary security and crowd control.
3. Arrange all necessary paperwork for administration on the day.
4. Confirm with all official personnel that they clearly understand what they are being required to do on the day.
5. Make all final arrangements.

Before the event

1. Ensure that all final arrangements are complete.
2. Arrange for signs to be available to direct participants to necessary areas.

On the day of the event

1. Run a final check to ensure everything is in order and ready to go.
2. Hold a brief meeting with all event personnel to confirm arrangements and make any last-minute alterations and answer any relevant queries.
3. Throughout the event keep in touch with all personnel and support them in their roles.
4. Deal with any crises that arise.

Immediately after the event

1. Prepare and send out an appropriate press release about the event.
2. Write necessary thankyou letters.
3. Start to chase up relevant accounts and pay bills.

A week to a month after the event

1. Report to participants.
2. Report to organisers.
3. Report to official personnel.
4. Report to relevant national bodies.
5. Draw up a concluding financial report.
6. Make any recommendations for future events.

A simple action list

Task	Who	With whom	When	Equipment	Other comments
Book venue	Venue director	Event manager	1 year in advance		Agree costs
Procure chairs and tables	Equipment director		9 months in advance	1000 chairs 500 tables	
Find necessary volunteer personnel	Personnel director	Equipment, stewarding and car parking directors	3–6 months in advance		No technical personnel

An implementation document

Having identified the requirements and worked out a timescale, we are now ready to produce a detailed implementation plan to get everything up and running. It may be simple, perhaps a single sheet of instructions to staff and volunteers; or it may be very complex, perhaps a collection of handbooks to VIP hosts, stewards, catering staff, etc., at an international event. But most events have a fairly routine implementation plan; it may be a simple checklist that shows who does what and by when. Here is an example.

Event requirement	Detail	Timescale	Undertaken by
Book venue	Confirm suitability Fix date	18 months ahead	Venue manager
Arrange main speaker	Sufficient standing in profession Pencil in alternatives	12 months ahead	Conference director
Arrange venue layout	Space for working groups as well as listening	3 months ahead	Venue manager
Confirm catering arrangement	Final confirmation after delegate numbers	1 month ahead	Catering manager

Timescale	2 years	18 months	1 year	6 months	3 months	1 month	Event	1 month after	3 months after
Event requirement									
Market research									
Secure finance									
Book venue									
Arrange catering									
First aid									
Safety check									
Detailed costing									

The next section contains two examples of a detailed event implementation document. Their approach is based on a system operated by the UK armed services for carrying out major military occasions like parades and state functions. It has been adapted for use in a major leisure facility, in order to keep staff informed of what has to be done, by whom and when, for an event to be achieved. Each document should be seen as a written confirmation of arrangements already made, placing them in order and informing staff of how the whole event fits together.

Many centres and events operate successfully with a much more basic checklist of things to be done. It is up to the event manager to decide on what is most appropriate in a particular situation, but any document must do two things:

● Indicate who is responsible for taking what action.

● Establish a timescale for the necessary actions.

Administrative instructions

ADMINISTRATIVE INSTRUCTION NO 80/9

**SPORTS FORUM, SEMINAR AND EXHIBITION PROGRAMME
10 AND 11 OCTOBER 199_**

Information

1 Date and Time

Thursday 10 October 1900–2100 hours approximately.
Sports Forum in the Dance Studio.

Friday 11 October 0915–1700 hours.
Seminar in the Dance Studio.

2 Venues

2.1 The exhibition area on the Gameshall Balcony (Appendix A).

2.2 The catering area will be the central area on the Gameshall Balcony (Appendix A).

2.3 Reading Room – Speakers Meeting Room with Discussion Area.

2.4 GP1 – Discussion Area for Seminar Workshop.

3 General

Approximately 100 delegates will attend the Seminar programme on Friday. The delegates represent Education and Recreation Departments from all areas of Scotland. For details of the Seminar and Exhibition programme see Appendices.

4 Reception

4.1 Reception of Speakers:
Thursday   Mr Watt
Friday   Mr Jack
On arrival, Session Chairman and Speakers will be met at the entrance and shown to the Reading Room for registration and final programme details. Coffee will be served in this area.

4.2 Reception for Delegates:
Thursday   Mr Stevenson, Mr Watt
Friday   Mr Watt, Mrs Henderson
Thursday Forum invitees should proceed to Gameshall Balcony for a welcome refreshment.

▷

On arrival on Friday, delegates are to be shown to the Gameshall Balcony where registration will be carried out.

4.3 Reception of Exhibitors on Thursday during the day:
Mr Stevenson, Mr Olivia, Mr Gibson

5 Appendices

Appendix A   Dance Studio Layout
Appendix B   Seminar Programme
Appendix C   Reception Detail
Appendix D   Catering Detail
Appendix E   Audiovisual Requirements
Appendix F   Reading Room and GP1 Layouts
Appendix G   Trades Exhibition

Preparation and Execution	**Action By**
6 Advance Preparation	
6.1 Gameshall and Balcony preparation and work prior to 1300 hours on Friday.	Mr Gibson Mr Oliva
– Mark out exhibition stand area with tape	Attendants
– Install electric supply for easy positioning of sockets from temporary supply	Mr Donnelly
– Position one Council banner on the Balcony railing	Attendants
– Check all Dance Studio curtains and <u>ensure total blackout is possible</u>	Mr Oliva Mr Gibson
6.2 *General*	
– Specially clean all glass in corridors, front entrance, Gameshall entrance and side stairs	General Assts
– Remove all untidy notices and replace as required with fresh notices (noticeboards, corridors, entrance doors, etc.)	Mr Donnelly
– Rehang curtains and blinds in Dance Studio, Reading Room and GP1	Attendants Mr Gibson Mr Oliva
– Remove, to store, all unnecessary equipment from corridors Dance Studio, Reading Room and GP1	Attendants Mr Gibson Mr Oliva
– Prepare display boards as per Appendix G	Mr Donnelly
– Obtain small stage section, carpet and lectern from GTC	Mr Oliva Mr Gibson
– Obtain 100 comfortable delegate chairs from Hotel	Mr Montague

– Specially clean canopy over main entrance and remove all litter from areas surrounding the Institute		Mr Oliva Mr Gibson Attendants
– All toilets to be specially cleaned immediately prior to 1900 hours on Wednesday, with facilities in the Social Area, stocked with ample supplies of soap and paper towels		Mr Oliva Mr Gibson Attendants

7 Gameshall Balcony

7.1	The floor area to be cleaned between 1000 and 1300 hours and floor tape markings finalised.	General Assts Attendants
7.2	Electric cables and sockets to be positioned around exhibition area. All cables to be taped to floor.	Mr Oliva Mr Gibson Attendants Mr Donnelly
7.3	Supply will have to come from the Gameshall (apparatus bay) and Social Area.	Mr Donnelly
7.4	Assist Exhibitors to move equipment into Exhibition Area and assist with display assembly as required.	Attendants
7.5	Position tables and chairs for stands, coffee and lunch areas as shown in Appendix A.	Attendants
7.6	PA system to be checked and operating over the programmed period on Thursday evening and Friday.	Mr Donnelly Mr Oliva Mr Gibson
7.7	PA system to be available for announcements throughout preparation and exhibition programme.	
7.8	Assist with movement and positioning of all plants as supplied; see Appendix A.	Attendants
7.9	Council prepared display stands to be in position by 1500 hours on Gameshall Balcony.	
7.10	Set up registration area in Gameshall for delegates, using two tables (Appendix A).	Attendants

8 Dance Studio

8.1	Area to be fully cleaned on Thursday 10 October and finally set up by 1700 hours.	Mr Oliva Mr Gibson General Assts
8.2	Staging suitably fitted with covering carpet and steps as shown in Appendix A.	Mr Oliva Mr Gibson Attendants

8.3	All seating to be positioned as per Appendix A – 10 chairs in three blocks and side passageways.	Attendants
8.4	All unnecessary equipment to be stored and the floor area free from extra equipment.	Attendants
8.5	AV equipment as requested plus screen.	Mr Donnelly
8.6	Provide table and chairs on stage as per Appendix A.	Mr Donnelly Attendants Mr Oliva Mr Gibson
8.7	Provide decanter and glasses for speakers.	Catering Staff
8.8	Provide and position lectern.	Mr Donnelly
8.9	Position staging, stage cover and steps as in Appendix A.	Mr Donnelly
8.10	Position troughs of flowers in front of stage (Appendix A).	DC Staff

9 Reading Room

9.1	All books and all magazine stands to be made tidy.	Mr Donnelly
9.2	Four large tables to be moved to Gameshall for buffet and coffee service tables.	Attendants
9.3	Four coffee tables each surrounded by five folding chairs to remain with three large tables for registration of speakers.	Attendants
9.4	On Thursday half the room is to be set up for a buffet meal for seven people by 1730 hours.	Attendants Mrs Hamilton
9.5	On Thursday at 2100 hours approximately, speakers and guests may return to this room for refreshments and coffee.	Attendants Mrs Hamilton
9.6	On Friday after 1000 hours this room is to be set with a top table and 30 chairs in rows for workshop session.	Attendants Mr Oliva Mr Gibson

10 GP1

10.1	On Thursday by 1700 hours GP1 has to be set up with two top tables and 50 chairs in rows for Friday workshops.	Attendants Mr Oliva Mr Gibson
10.2	A video playback facility has to be placed in this room on Friday by 1000 hours.	Mr Donnelly

▷

11 Floral Decorations

11.1 Two table decorations to be provided and made available in dining area.	Parks Dept
11.2 Two troughs of flowers to be provided for front of stage in Dance Studio.	Parks Dept

12 Toilets

12.1 Toilets are to be cleaned and made fresh several times on both the Thursday and Friday. Ample supplies of soap and paper towels are to be provided.	Attendants
12.2 The wastepaper bins in toilets and throughout the building are to be emptied several times throughout the day.	Attendants
12.3 Fresh air spray to be used on frequent occasions.	Attendants
12.4 All toilets fittings, hand basins, etc., are to be specially cleaned.	Attendants

13 Grounds

13.1 Special attention is to be given to ensure that the Centre grounds and pathways around the building are free from litter.	Attendants Groundsman
13.2 St Andrew's flag, Union Jack, Council Flag and Year of Sport Flag are to be flown on Thursday night and Friday throughout the Forum and Seminar programme.	Pool Super.

14 Corridor Control

14.1 Attendants are to supervise the corridor outside the Dance Studio and keep passing noise to a minimum on Thursday evening and Friday seminar session.	Attendants

Distribution

Mr J S Oliva	Mr S Donnelly
Mr R Gibson	Mrs J Henderson
Attendants (3)	Mrs F Smith
Supervisor	Senior Staff
Catering Staff	Parks Dept
General Assistant	File
Reception Staff (2)	

DCW/MS
October 199_

APPENDIX A

Dance Studio Layout

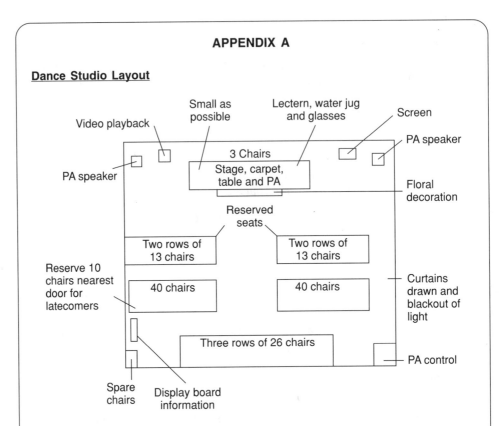

APPENDIX B

Seminar Programme

9.30 am	Coffee and Exhibition	
10.00 am	Welcome and Introduction	Chairman, ILAM Scotland
10.10 am	FUTURE LEISURE TRENDS	Kit Campbell (Kit Campbell Associates)
10.45 am	Discussion	
11.00 am	WORKSHOPS	
	Encouraging Participation	Maureen Campbell (Scottish Sports Council)
	Women in Sport	Leonora Nicol (Kirkcaldy District Council) Maureen Clowe (Scottish Keep Fit Assoc.)
	Quality Leadership	
12.00 pm	Lunch and Exhibition	Immediate Past Chairman (ILAM Scotland)
1.30 pm	Introduction by David Arnott	
1.40 pm	TEAM SPORT SCOTLAND INITIATIVE	Director, Team Sport Scotland

2.30 pm	WORKSHOPS	Gerry Ralph
	Club Junior Development	(Kelburne Hockey Club)
	Initiatives	Douglas Arneill
	National Governing Body Role	(Scottish Rugby Union)
	What is Happening in Schools	Charles Raeburn(FOSSSA)
3.30 pm	ILAM Roadshow	Director of Education and Training (ILAM)
	Workshop	
	sport Opportunities for Elderly People	Dorothy Dobson (Dundee University)
4.30 pm	Dispersal	

APPENDIX C

Reception Detail

1 Reception of Guest and Speakers

Thursday   Mr Watt
Friday   Mr Jack

1.1 On arrival speakers are to be shown to the Reading Room, where coffee will be available on Friday morning. A special meal is being prepared for speakers at 5.30 pm on Thursday.

1.2 Each speaker is to be issued with an information pack including badge (badge to be displayed for entry to conference, lunch and coffee area).

1.3 A member of staff to be available to escort any guests or speakers to the Reading Room.

1.4 All guests to be advised
   • they will be asked to sit in the reserved area at the front of the hall until invited on to the stage
   • all speakers and the platform party to move to the Dance Studio no later than 6.55 pm on Thursday and 9.55 am on Friday

1.5 Late arrivals will be met at Reception and escorted to the Reading Room to collect papers before being shown to the Dance Studio.

2 Reception of Delegates

Thursday   Mr Watt, Mr Stevenson
Friday   Mr Watt, Mrs Henderson

Registration Area within Gameshall Balcony

2.1 All delegates have to register on arrival.

2.2 Delegates are to be issued with information pack and badge.
   Note: Each delegate must be advised to retain and display badge as it is accepted as the pass into the coffee, lunch and

seminar areas. The badge issued on Thursday is to be retained for use on Friday as appropriate.

2.3 On the Registration Sheet staff are to record attendance and indicate with the letters AC <u>if an attendance certificate is required</u>. Indicate days, Thursday and/or Friday. When this is requested, delegates are to be advised that they may collect an attendance certificate from the Reception in the Entrance Hall after 1.30 pm.

2.4 On Friday ask delegates which workshop they wish to visit.

2.5 Advise delegates that coffee will be provided in the Gameshall area at no charge (badge display only required).

2.6 Advise delegates of the location of cloakroom facilities, e.g. clothes retention in the pool basketroom. Toilets are located on the first floor in the Social Area or beside the viewing balcony of the pool area.

3 Reception of Exhibitors

Mr Stevenson

3.1 On arrival exhibitors are to be issued with information packs, which will include a badge.

3.2 They are to be advised that the pack contains a complimentary lunch ticket. If they require additional lunch tickets they may be purchased for £2.50 from the Cafeteria. (All cash collected is to be passed to Mr Stevenson for coding to the Catering Income Code.)

3.3 Coffee is available, at no charge, to all the exhibitors in the <u>Gameshall Balcony Area</u>.

3.4 Wine and glasses will be issued by Mr Stevenson.

3.5 It is not intended that the stands need to be manned during the seminar sessions, only during the coffee and lunch periods, as per programme.

APPENDIX D

<u>Catering Detail</u>

Action By

1 Thursday Evening

		Action By
1.1	A buffet meal for eight people to be set out in the Reading Room by 5.30 pm.	Mrs Hamilton Mr Stevenson
1.2	Wine has to accompany this meal.	Mrs Hamilton Mr Stevenson
1.3	Wine and coffee, and a finger buffet is to be available for invitees on the Gameshall Balcony by 6 pm.	Mrs Hamilton Mr Stevenson

2 Lunch

2.1 Buffet lunch to be prepared and set up on Friday by 12 pm.   Mrs Hamilton

2.2 Exhibitors (approx. 10 lunches) to be served early (approx. 11.30 am) on each day.   Mrs Hamilton

2.3 Lunch is to be provided only on receipt of lunch ticket vouchers.   Mrs Smith

One member of staff to collect <u>all</u> lunch vouchers (including exhibitors, delegates, staff and guests).   Mrs Hamilton

All tickets to be retained and passed to Mr Stevenson after they have been counted for accounting purposes.   Mrs Hamilton

3 Coffee

3.1 Coffee and biscuits will be required during registration and reception from 9.30 am to 10.15 am on each day (available from a central exhibition point).   Mrs Hamilton

3.2 Coffee to be available from a central exhibition point throughout the day.   Mrs Hamilton

3.3 A large demand for coffee after lunch on each day, available from a central exhibition point.   Mrs Hamilton

3.4 Tea and coffee in limited numbers (approx. 40) will be required on dispersal at 4.15 pm on Friday to be served from trolley in Reading Room.   Mrs Hamilton

4 Reading Room

Available from 4 pm to be specially tidied, curtains hung, etc., and set out as below for a buffet meal for eight people at 6 pm.   Mr Gibson
Mr Oliva
Attendants

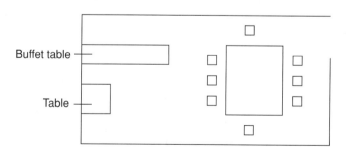

4.1 Buffet to consist of three courses (including wine) and coffee. Waitress assistance is required.   Mrs Hamilton

4.2 To be prepared and ready to serve from 5.30 pm.   Mrs Hamilton

5 Gameshall Balcony

To be set up per reception of guests by 5.45 pm. Wine,   Mrs Hamilton
soft drinks and finger buffet to be served.

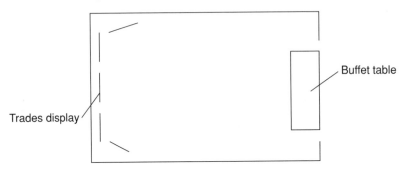

Trades display

Buffet table

5.1 Balcony to be cleared of all unnecessary equipment,   Mr Gibson
     and specially cleaned and tidied.   Mr Oliva
                                                               Attendants

6 Evening Refreshment

Reading Room to be cleared, and coffee and refreshment   Mrs Hamilton
available from about 8.15 pm.

APPENDIX E

Audiovisual Requirements

                                                               Action By

1 Promotion

1.1 Three display boards carrying current information   Mr Donnelly
     material to be prepared.   Senior Staff
     Backup brochure information to be available on small
     tables erected on Gameshall Balcony, as per layout,
     and in Dance Studio.

1.2 (a) Selection of slides featuring activity in and around Mr Donnelly
         Centre to be prepared, shown in Gameshall
         Balcony area.
     (b) Video selection of centre activities to be prepared, Mr Donnelly
         shown in Gameshall Balcony area.

1.3 All notices, whiteboards and general public information   Mr Donnelly
     to be checked, tidied and updated as necessary by
     Wednesday 9 October.

2 Seminar Backup

2.1 PA system to be set up and checked.   Mr Donnelly

2.2 Audio record to made of all sessions.   Mr Donnelly

2.3 Overhead projector, screen, video playback, flip chart and pens, and slide projector to be available as required by speakers in Dance Studio, Reading Room and GP1.   Mr Donnelly

2.4 Video and photographic record to be made.   Mr Donnelly

2.5 Two additional overhead projectors, plus bulbs and pens are required for Friday's workshop in Reading Room and GP2.   Mr Donnelly

3 Notices

3.1 Directional notices (with logos added) are to be placed in the front foyer and the rear entrance.   Mr Donnelly

3.2 Toilets are all to be clearly marked.   Mr Donnelly

3.3 A sign has to be made for the Registration Desk.   Mr Donnelly

3.4 Notice to be placed on the front noticeboard by 9 am Wednesday 9 October: Rec. Office

SCOTTISH SPORTS FORUM
DANCE STUDIO
WEDNESDAY 10 OCTOBER AT 7.00 PM

And on Thursday 10th October after 9.00 pm:

ILAM SCOTLAND SEMINAR
DANCE STUDIO
FRIDAY 11 OCTOBER 10.00 AM

3.5 QUIET PLEASE SEMINAR IN PROGRESS notices to be placed at either end of the downstairs corridor on Thursday evening and Friday all day.   Mr Donnelly

APPENDIX F

READING ROOM AND GP1 LAYOUTS

Reading Room

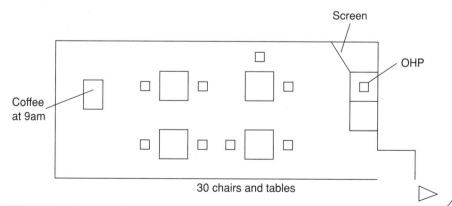

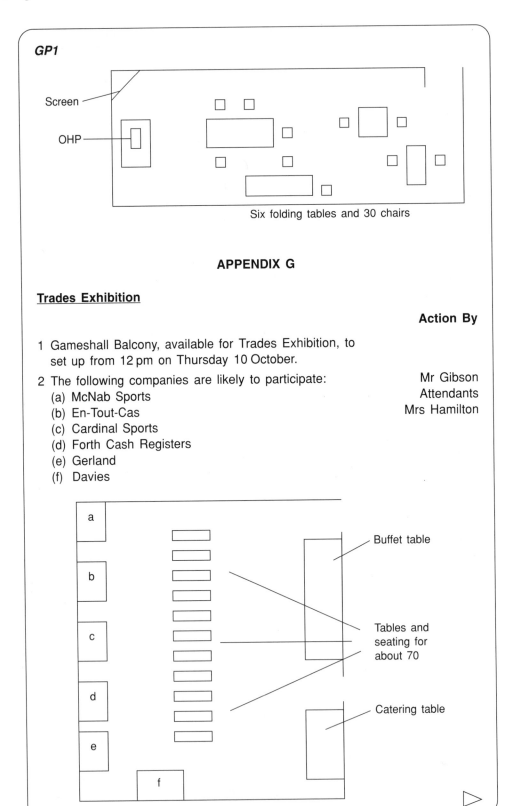

GP1

Screen

OHP

Six folding tables and 30 chairs

APPENDIX G

Trades Exhibition

Action By

1 Gameshall Balcony, available for Trades Exhibition, to set up from 12 pm on Thursday 10 October.

2 The following companies are likely to participate:
    Mr Gibson
    Attendants
    Mrs Hamilton
  (a) McNab Sports
  (b) En-Tout-Cas
  (c) Cardinal Sports
  (d) Forth Cash Registers
  (e) Gerland
  (f) Davies

a

b

c

d

e

f

Buffet table

Tables and seating for about 70

Catering table

NB Central tables for catering to be set up from 10 am on Friday 11 October.

1 This area is to be used for reception and coffee from 9 am on Friday 11 October.

2 Area to be set up for lunch from 10 am; lunch is served at 12 pm. Coffee available in Reading Room from 4 pm.

ADMINISTRATIVE INSTRUCTION NO: 93/09

WHAT'S NEXT FOR WOMEN EXHIBITION

Information

1 Date and Time

Preparation

Monday 13 November	2000–2300 hours:	Courts 1–6
	2100–2300 hours:	Whole Hall, Dance Studio, GP1 and GP2
Tuesday 14 November	0900–1200 hours:	All Facilities

Exhibition

Tuesday 14 November	1330–1600 hours and 1800–2030 hours
Wednesday 15 November	0930–1200 hours, 1330–1600 hours and 1800–2030 hours
Thursday 16 November	0930–1200 hours and 1330–1600 hours

Restoration of Gameshall

Thursday 16 November	1600–1800 hours

2 Venue

Whole Gameshall and Balcony, GP1 and GP2, Dance Studio, Squash Courts (Wednesday only), Fitness Room (Wednesday evening only), Social Area, Reading Room (Wednesday afternoon and evening only) and All-Weather Area.

3 General

This is a Careers Convention and Exhibition aimed exclusively at women. It particularly aims to encourage women into unusual and innovative careers.

4 Appendices

Appendix A	Gameshall Layout
Appendix B	Balcony and Social Area Layout
Appendix C	Equipment Requirements

Appendix D	Catering Requirements
Appendix E	Notices
Appendix F	Transport Schedule
Appendix G	Location of Activities
Appendix H	Timetable
Appendix I	Exhibitors

Preparation and Execution   **Action By**

5 Advance Preparation

(a) Power supply as required to be identified.   Mr Watt
                                                                         Mr Don
                                                                         Mr Oliva

(b) All equipment as required in Appendix A to be   Mr Don
     arranged and transported to the Institute.   Mr Oliva
                                                                         Mr Donnelly

(c) All notices as per Appendix E are to be   Mr Donnelly
     prepared.

(d) Boards, brochures and handouts publicising the   Mrs Coull
     work of the Centre are to be prepared.   Mr Donnelly
                                                                         Mr Stevenson

(e) All Centre noticeboards and display cabinets are   Mr Stevenson
     to be cleared and cleaned as necessary, then to
     be arranged with comprehensive publicity on the
     work of the Centre.

(f) Additional power cables and sockets to be   Mr Donnelly
     purchased and coded to the event.

(g) All electrical and other Council equipment to be   All Staff
     clearly marked and closely guarded.

(h) A regional electrician to come and connect ring   Mr Oliva
     power circuit to Gameshall.   Mr Don
                                                                         Mr Donnelly
(i) At least half of the Centre's floor covering to be
     brought to the Gameshall apparatus bay.

6 Gameshall, Balcony and Social Area

   *6.1 Preparation on Monday 13 November at
        2000–2300 hours*
        (a) Five-a-side boards to be placed on side   Attendants
             CD store.

▷

(b) Two small bleachers to be placed back to back with large bleachers in present position. — Attendants

(c) One small bleacher to be placed on either side of the Gameshall entrance, opened out and cleaned. — Attendants

(d) Floor covering to form walkways as illustrated on Appendix A. — Attendants

(e) Exhibition stands to be allocated and marked out. — Ms Holland

(f) Ring circuit to be set out and power lead to be brought from the balcony and from the roof. — Mr Oliva / Mr Don

(g) It is <u>essential</u> that all the many power cables required are <u>taped to the floor or taped to a rope from the roof</u> and at <u>all times made totally safe.</u> — All Staff

(h) All tables and chairs for exhibitors to be placed at a central point in the hall for late collection.

6.2 Preparation on Tuesday 14 November at 0900–1200 hours

(a) Exhibitors will arrive and set up their displays within the area allocated and marked out for them. — Ms Holland

(b) All other final preparations are to be made ready for the official opening at 1315 hours. — All Staff

(c) Care has to be taken that the entrance through the fire doors for the All-Weather Area is kept as clean as possible to avoid bringing dirt into the Hall. — Attendants

(d) During periods of Exhibition closure, close supervision has to be given for all areas: — All Staff

Lunchtime   1200–1330 hours
Teatime   1600–1800 hours
Overnight   2030–0930 hours

Especially overnight, all possible doors are to be locked and valuable items are to be removed to a safe area.

(e) Fire doors must be open during the day but securely locked at night. — Mr Don / Mr Oliva / Attendants

▷

7 All-Weather Area

(a) Layout

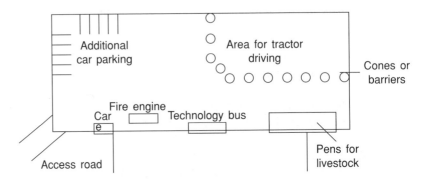

(b) This area will be used as an extension of the exhibition area, for some items which cannot go into the Hall and for excess car parking.

All Staff

(c) On Monday 13 November the area should be rolled, brushed and tidied.

Groundsman

(d) On Friday 17 November it needs to be brushed and tidied again to restore any minor damage.

Groundsman

8 Garage

(a) During the three days, and Tuesday and Wednesday night, the garage will be required for storage of the animal pens and the tractor.

Mr Oliva
Mr Don
Attendants

(b) The Centre minibus is to be parked nose into the back of the swimming-pool during this time.

Mr Montague

9 Crèche – GP2

(a) During the period of the exhibition the crèche will run in GP2.

All Staff

(b) It will run as follows
Tuesday   0900–1200   1330–1600   1800–2030
Wednesday 0900–1200   1330–1600   1800–2030
Thursday   0900–1200   1330–1600

(c) Admission will be free of charge.

All Staff

(d) All equipment has to be moved from GP1 and set up in GP2.

Creche Staff
Attendants

(e) Equipment may be left out in this area until 1600 hours on Thursday, then it must be returned to GP1.

Creche Staff
Attendants

10 GP1

(a) This room will be used for workshop sessions.

(b) It is to be set up as follows:

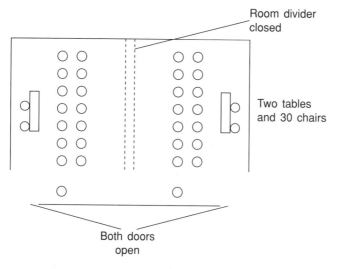

Room divider closed

Two tables and 30 chairs

Both doors open

11 Upper Floor

(a) Videos are to be shown in this area.

Ms Holland

(b) Where there are no staff overnight in this area, the equipment will be placed in the Advance Booking Office and played out of the window.

Mr Donnelly

12 Squash Courts

(a) One court will be used for a theatre technical workshop all day Wednesday. The other for a self-defence session on Wednesday evening.

(b) One court to have one table and 15 chairs (all with pads on legs).

Attendants

(c) Great care to be taken over footwear worn in these courts, especially high-heeled shoes.

All Staff

13 Fitness Testing Room (Old)

(a) This room needs to be used on Wednesday, daytime and evening, for workshops.

(b) It requires a table and 15 chairs.

14 Reading Room

(a) This room will be used on Wednesday all day for workshops.

(b) The large tables (except one) can be removed to the Dance Studio on Tuesday.

Attendants

(c) One large table and 15 chairs are required for workshops.

All Staff

15 Dance Studio

This room requires several prompt changes throughout the exhibition and it must be kept tidy at all times and be clear of unnecessary items.

All Staff

(a) *Launch Lunch*
This buffet lunch for approx. 25 will be held on Tuesday 1200–1315 hours.

Attendants
Catering Staff

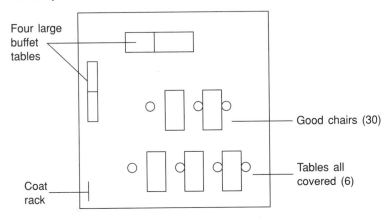

Four large buffet tables

Good chairs (30)

Tables all covered (6)

Coat rack

(b) *Industrial Seminar*
This session for Industrialists and Officials with a finger buffet is to be held on Tuesday 1900–2030 hours.

Attendants
Catering Staff

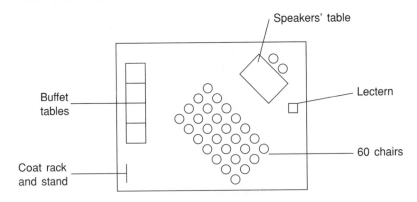

Speakers' table

Buffet tables

Lectern

60 chairs

Coat rack and stand

(c) *Drama Presentation*

(i) The production Millie's Dream will be presented in the Dance Studio:

Wednesday 1230, 1830 and 1900 hours
Thursday 1230 hours

(ii) The set-up for this will be on Wednesday 0900–1200 hours.

Attendants
Cast

(iii)   Layout for this will be as follows:

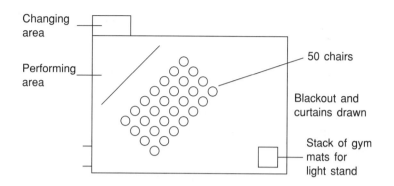

Changing area

Performing area

50 chairs

Blackout and curtains drawn

Stack of gym mats for light stand

(iv)	The store will be required as a changing area. Equipment should be removed on Wednesday morning to the other store.	Attendants
(v)	Four heavy weights are to be provided to help with the weighing down of light stands.	Attendants
(d) (i)	During Wednesday afternoon the journalists workshops will be held in the Dance Studio.	Attendants
(ii)	Some of the show seating is to be turned round and four tables are to be provided as follows:	

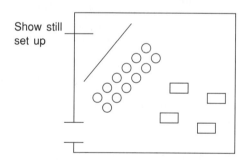

Show still set up

16 Floodlit Grass Football Pitch

(a)	As part of the Exhibition, a ladies' football match will take place under floodlights on Tuesday at 1930–2100 hours.	All Staff
	Central Ladies v United Social Club	
(b)	The pitch is to be marked, and nets and corners flagged out.	Groundsman
(c)	These nets and flags to be brought in by teams and staff.	Attendants

(d) The Ladies' Gameshall Changing Rooms are to be issued to teams.

Attendants

DCW/MS
November 199_

Distribution

Mr Don	Groundsman
Mr Oliva	Crèche Staff
Mr Donnelly	Senior Staff
Mr Watt (2)	Teaching Staffroom
Mr Montage (Driver)	Teaching Staff
Mrs Coull	Miss Allison
Pool Supervisor	Recreation Office
Mrs Hamilton	Attendants (2)
Catering Staff	Careers Services (via D C Watt)
Ms Holland	

APPENDIX A

Gameshall Layout

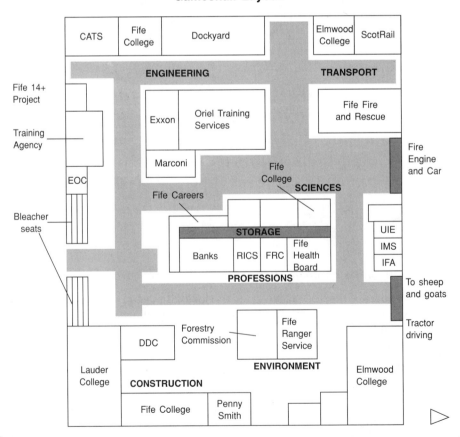

APPENDIX B

Gameshall Balcony and Social Area Layout

Behind Balcony

Balcony

Social area

CATS

SWAP

Photographic
competition

Fife
College

Adult
Support
Unit

Glenrothes
College

TAP

Viewforth
High
School

▷

APPENDIX C

Equipment Requirements

	Action By
1 Additional extension cable and six 4-outlet sockets to be purchased.	Mr Donnelly
2 320 chairs, 25 easy chairs and 130 tables (3 ft × 3 ft) are required for Gameshall and rooms; to be obtained from various sources and brought to the Centre.	Mr Oliva Mr Don
3 All Centre noticeboards and display cabinets will be needed to publicise the work of the Centre.	Mr Donnelly
4 Dance Studio curtains will require to be in as good a condition as possible.	Mr Oliva Mr Don
5 Video and photographs to be taken. Equipment to be available and working.	Mr Donnelly
6 Viewdata screens to be working and include information on Appendices F, G, H and L.	Mr Donnelly

APPENDIX D

Catering Requirements

	Action By
1 There is to be a Launch Lunch in the Dance Studio at 1200–1315 hours on Tuesday 14 November. This will be a buffet for around 25, of high-calibre provision, including wine for about £5.00 per head.	Mrs Hamilton Catering Staff Mr Stevenson
2 An Industrial Seminar is to be held on Tuesday 14 November at 1900–2030 hours. There is to be a finger buffet, including wine, for around 50 people at £2.50 a head.	Mr Stevenson
3 Over the three days the exhibitors and staff will eat lunch and tea in the restaurant. They will submit tickets at value £2.00 each; additional cost will be to the individual.	Mr Stevenson Ms Holland
4 Four hundred meal tickets to be produced and given to Mr Watt. They should contain the event logo.	Mrs Coull

---

What's Next for Women?

Meal Ticket £2.00

---

5 The restaurant is to open at 0900 hours each day for early arrivals to the event.	Mrs Hamilton Mr Stevenson
6 An urn of hot water, 100 polystyrene cups, coffee, tea, milk, sugar and biscuits are to be placed in the apparatus bay on side AB by the sink. This has to be replenished regularly and kept stocked from 0900 hours Tuesday to 1600 hours Thursday.	Mr Stevenson

APPENDIX E

Notices

Action By

1 Information on this event to be put on the front foyer noticeboard from Friday 10 November.	Recreation Office
2 Posters for the event to be widely displayed throughout the building from Wednesday 8 November. They must go on every entrance door, plus windows and noticeboards.	Mr Donnelly
3 All notices for the event are to feature the event logo.	Mr Donnelly
4 Directional notices to the Exhibition are to be placed in the front and rear foyer and at the base of all stairs directing patrons to the Gameshall.	Mr Donnelly
5 Notices saying ADDITIONAL STANDS are needed to direct patrons to the Gameshall Balcony and the Social Area.	Mr Donnelly
6 Notices to be prepared for workshops as follows and placed as per Appendix G:	Ms Holland

WHAT'S NEXT FOR WOMEN WORKSHOP
MANAGEMENT SWAP MATHS PHYSICS
CONFIDENCE THEATRE TECHNICAL SELF-DEFENCE
FITNESS TRAINING DRAMA SHOW FRC

7 WHAT'S NEXT FOR WOMEN	Mr Donnelly

Toilets Crèche Café

Notice to be prepared for the door of GP2 and notices
in foyers to direct people to these services.

8 Twenty spare blank posters to be prepared.

APPENDIX F

Transport Schedule

A minibus will run at the following times from the Leisure Centre (rear entrance) to the Careers Information Office at Albany House in the Town Centre. This service will be free.

Tuesday and Wednesday Evening

Leave Careers Office   1745
Leave Centre   1800

And so on every 15 min until

Leave Careers Office   2015
Leave Centre   2030

Wednesday Afternoon

Leave Careers Office   1345
Leave Centre   1400

And so on every 15 min until

Leave Careers Office   1545
Leave Centre   1600

Other services will be added if possible.

APPENDIX G

Location of Activities

Gameshall	Exhibition	Monday night Tuesday am, pm, evening Wednesday am, pm, evening Thursday am, pm
Gameshall	Exhibition	As above
Balcony	Exhibition	As above
Social Area	Management Workshop	Wednesday pm, evening
Fitness Testing	SWAP Workshop	Wednesday pm, evening
Room (Old)	Journalism Workshop	Wednesday am
Reading Room	FRC Workshops	Wednesday pm, evening
	Broadcast Workshop	Time unknown
Room Unknown	Launch Lunch	Tuesday lunchtime
Dance Studio	Industrial Seminar	Tuesday evening
	Drama Show	Wednesday am (prep) Wednesday 1230 (performance)

▷

Dance Studio	Journalism Workshop	Wednesday pm
	Drama Show	Wednesday 1630
		(performance)
		Wednesday 1930
		(performance)
		Thursday 1230
		(performance)
GP2	Crèche	Tuesday am, pm, evening
		Wednesday am, pm, evening
		Thursday am, pm
GP1	Maths Workshop	All times
	Physics Workshop	All times
	Confidence Workshop	All times
Upper Foyer (Advance Booking Office)	Videos	All times
Squash Courts	Theatre Technical Workshop	Wednesday am, pm, evening
	Self-Defence Class	Wednesday evening
Fitness Room	Fitness Class	Wednesday evening
All-Weather Area	Exhibition and Parking	All times
Floodlit Grass Park	Ladies' Football Match	Wednesday evening

APPENDIX H

Timetable

Monday

| 2000–2300 | Set-up |

Tuesday

0800–1315	Set-up
1200–1315	Launch Lunch
1315–1330	Opening Speeches
1330–1600	Public Exhibition, School Parties, one S2 Workshop
1800–2030	Public Exhibition, Parents & Women
1900–2030	Three Women's Workshops
1900–2030	Seminar: Facing Up to the Future

Wednesday

0900–0930	Preparation
0930–1200	Public Exhibition, School Parties, two S2 Workshops, five S3–S6 Workshops
1230–1300	Millie's Dream

▷

1330–1600	Public Exhibition, School Parties, two S2 Workshops, five S3–S6 Workshops
1800–2030	Public Exhibition, Parents & Women
1830–1900	Millie's Dream
1900–1930	Millie's Dream
1900–2030	Eight Women's Workshops

Thursday

0900–0930	Preparation
0930–1200	Public Exhibition, School Parties, two S2 Workshops, five S3–S6 Workshops
1230–1300	Millie's Dream
1330–1600	Public Exhibition, School Parties, two S2 Workshops, five S3–S6 Workshops
1600 onwards	Dismantling and Clear-up

APPENDIX I

Exhibitors

Upstairs

	Computing		
2	10	17	32
up	27	1	29

Main hall

17	10	23	5	25
	Engineering		Transport	
8	7	22		11
30	21			
6			Sciences 10	31
	9	Professions		19
	26	24 15 12		18
	4	16 14		
20 Construction		Environment	5	
3	10	28	4	

Key

1 Adult Support Unit
2 Computer Assisted Training Services (CATS)

 3 Construction Industry Training Board
 4 Dunfermline District Council
 5 Elmwood College
 6 Equal Opportunities Commission
 7 Exxon Chemical Olefins Inc
 8 Fife 14+ Project
 9 Fife Careers Service
10 Fife College of Technology
11 Fife Fire and Rescue Service
12 Fife Health Board
13 Fife Institute of Physical and Recreational Education
14 Fife Ranger Service
15 Fife Regional Council
16 Forestry Commission
17 Glenrothes College
18 Institute of Financial Accountants
19 Institute of Management Services
20 Lauder College
21 Marconi Instruments
22 Oriel Training Services
23 Rosyth Royal Dockyard
24 Royal Institution of Chartered Surveyors
25 ScotRail
26 Scottish Clearing Banks
27 Scottish Wider Access Programme
28 Penny Smith (woodworker)
29 Training Access Points (TAP)
30 Training Agency
31 University of Edinburgh and Institute of Physics
32 Viewforth High School

Chapter Eight

Sources of Help, Advice and Support

Many people get involved in event management almost by accident – through voluntary involvement or a change of job role – probably as many as those who consciously make career moves into the field. For anyone coming to event organisation, it is quite common that they will, at least initially, feel confused and alone. This is due to a shortage of training and also to the feelings of insecurity which characterise event management. (Have I done everything?) It is difficult to get a great deal of information, even from people who have been heavily involved; that's why I decided to write a book. The lack of information is partly because so many events have little written information that can be passed on, and partly because many experiences are still individual.

Remember, though, that few projects are totally novel or unique. It is very likely that someone has already done something similar to your venture, if not the same. Identifying them and picking their brains is going to make your task much easier and probably more successful. It is always better to learn from the mistakes of others, instead of your own. Take time to listen; most event organisers are only too happy to relate the details of their experiences. It is foolish to overlook their wisdom.

The enthusiasm and camaraderie of event organisers is one of the most supportive influences around. It will help others keep motivated even when they face an apparently insurmountable crisis. It is always nice to know that others have faced the same problems, and probably have a solution. This 'voluntary' support of colleagues from all aspects of the leisure field is a network which should be maintained and exploited. Some of the people who lent support to this publication (see the acknowledgements) might be a good place to start.

Professional help

For almost all events, there are bound to be areas where any individual or group of organisers lack experience or specialist knowledge. Sometimes this can be gleaned from other organisers or relevant contacts. However, it may also be wise to enlist professional help to cover any identified gap. There are several areas where paid commitment, definitive accuracy and guaranteed service are worth paying for. It is an investment for security and success, and brings in expertise where it is needed. Here are some of them:

- financial accounting and control
- legal issues
- health and safety
- insurance considerations
- medical support
- information technology
- technical expertise
- marketing
- emergency services

These are all areas where spending money to guarantee service delivery and secure professional knowledge may be beneficial. In some cases, like health and safety, it will often be obligatory.

Up-to-date information technology advice, as well as legal and financial matters are commonly in need of additional support. They are seldom the specialist areas of people staging events; event organisers may be experts in sports, arts, tourism or heritage, but rarely tie their enthusiasm to meticulous bookkeeping or extensive legal expertise. The number of firms offering services in these areas is expanding rapidly. Consultancies are growing up throughout the United Kingdom designed to move in and out of organisations providing professional help and support. This type of short-term input is often ideal for project managers, bringing in assistance only as required, for specific issues over limited timescales.

Law and insurance

Legal advice and insurance cover are sometimes downgraded or ignored completely. This can be extremely dangerous. From the early days of the organisation, there should be insurance to cover all possible contingencies. Among other areas, possible legal liabilities (to customers and staff) and potential loss of profit (consequential loss) should be carefully considered. Although it can be expensive, it is advisable to insure against cancellation and other crises; that is besides all the standard insurance cover, e.g. public and personal liability, personal accident, medical cover, mechanical failure, theft and fire. There are one or two very reputable firms in this area and it is advisable to go to a company that specialises in events (e.g. Insurex Exposure or GM Imber).

The importance of checking out all the negative possibilities cannot be overemphasised, yet it tends to be forgotten, perhaps because it appears so pessimistic. A lengthy discussion with a knowledgeable insurance broker, going through all possible eventualities, is time well spent and may save considerable heartache later on.

Over recent years most Western societies have seen a dramatic increase in the amount of legislation relating to customer and employee rights, health care and safety. These developments have obvious implications for events and suggest that legal advice is increasingly necessary. The no win, no fee lawyers have arrived and their existence threatens event organisers along with everybody else. So if in doubt, check it out! Here are some relevant items of UK legislation:

- The Occupiers Liability Acts 1957 and 1984
- The Employers Liability (Compulsory Insurance) Act 1960
- The Unfair Contract Terms Act 1977
- The Employment Protection Act 1978
- The Employment Act 1982
- The Health and Safety at Work Act 1974
- Office, Shops and Railway Premises Act 1963
- Health and Safety (First Aid) Regulations 1981

- The Equal Pay Act 1970
- The Wages Act 1986
- The Sex Discrimination Act 1975
- The Race Relations Act 1976
- The Public Health Acts 1875, 1890, 1907, 1925, 1936 and 1961
- The Open Services Act 1976
- The Defective Premises Act 1972
- The Sale of Goods Act 1979
- The Fire Precautions Act 1971
- The Fair Trading Act 1973
- The Consumer Safety Act 1978
- The Consumer Protection Act 1978
- The Supply of Goods and Services Act 1982
- The Trade Descriptions Acts 1968 and 1972
- The Betting, Gaming and Lotteries Act 1963 (and associated legislation)
- The Safety of Sports Grounds Act 1975 (and the Taylor Report 1990)
- The Licensing Act 1964, as amended by the Licensing Act 1988
- The Derelict Land Act 1982
- The Countryside Act 1968
- The Town and Country Planning Act 1990
- The Water Resources Act 1991
- The National Parks and Access to Countryside Act 1949
- The Wildlife and Countryside Act 1981
- The Gaming Act 1968
- The Private Places of Entertainment (Licensing) Act 1967

Quite a substantial list! And there are many more significant items of legislation and codes of practice to be considered, as well as new laws that seem to be enacted almost daily. There are overall considerations like performing rights, copyright, negligence, contributing negligence, liquor licensing, catering rules, public entertainment and fire regulations. These are set in a framework of general Acts of Parliament on local authorities, education, public health, health and safety, etc., as well as local authority by-laws.

Then there are specific orders on public halls, museums, libraries, art galleries, swimming-pools, etc. Add to that the founding Acts of the Arts Councils, Sports Councils, tourism authorities, and countryside bodies, not to mention the differences between Scottish and English law, include all relevant British and European Standards, and it creates a massive corpus of knowledge, unlikely to be possessed by most event organisers. Money spent ensuring that the correct legal procedures are followed is worthwhile and could well be a real saving in the long term.

Medical services

The need for medical support can vary enormously between events: from a couple of first aiders at the local fete to a large team of consultants, GPs, nurses, physiotherapists, etc.,

at a major international sporting event. Whatever the event, it is essential to have the appropriate medical cover based on expert advice about what is needed; don't ever be caught short of the required standard. A separate group or individual with responsibility solely for this area is normally the best practice. Here are some areas to consider:

- staffing level, paid and/or voluntary
- qualifications and number of staff
- the nature of the participants and their medical history
- emergency backup
- 'routine' illnesses, e.g. allergies and tummy bugs
- payment arrangements for foreign visitors
- diet
- ambulance availability
- age of participants
- doctor availability
- sports injury treatment
- general health provision
- medical and first-aid equipment
- cover for all areas, e.g. accommodation and event venues
- spectator control

Event organisation agencies

A relatively recent development has been the rapid increase in the emergence of firms who specialise in event or project management. Locally and nationally, companies are recognising the opportunity for making a significant commercial return by staging a major leisure happening in a whole variety of situations.

The business opportunity was identified very soon after government (local and national), industry and many voluntary bodies in the leisure sphere spotted how events can be significant. Events now seem to be crucial to tourism, arts, heritage or sports development initiatives, so there is a potentially worthwhile market for people, with the necessary knowledge and proficiency, to sell their skills to interested parties. This area of work will undoubtedly continue to grow as the importance of events becomes more widely recognised and as additional agencies, like enterprise councils, use events to implement their policies.

Hiring in professional expertise is not cheap (ranging upwards from £250 a day). It can often be sensible to set a fixed fee, negotiated before the work is undertaken as well as specifying certain performance measures at the outset. This can be useful to organisers for planning and budgeting – no blank cheques – and it guarantees that all work in a specific area will be done. In some areas, like sponsorship, it is possible to pay by results, i.e. on commission, say 20% of monies brought in. This can be extremely effective in ensuring hard work by the searching agency; if they don't earn any money, they don't get any. But bear in mind that having no sponsorship might kill off your event, though the agency can survive on other projects.

For the larger major events, professional help is really essential, although some means will need to be found to pay for it. Be sure to get references for the professionals; speak to people who have used them before, ensure their credentials are bona fide, and satisfy yourself they can deliver thier promises at an acceptable price.

Other agencies

Later in this appendix there is a list of useful addresses for leisure event organisers. They include national agencies like the Sports Councils and the Arts Councils along with national tourist authorities; professional institutes like the Institute of Leisure and Amenity Management, the Institute of Sport and Recreation Management and the National Outdoor Events Association; as well as other organisations which can supply information, reading, education courses, practical contacts and technical expertise. Local authorities are rather undervalued as a resource, yet they can often assist enormously in organising events.

Research and experience has shown there are few single agencies which can give all the necessary advice. However, by contacting a series of organisations relevant to a specific event, a great deal of very helpful information can be obtained. Again the commonality of the event is to be remembered. It is quite possible for an arts event organiser to learn from someone in the sports field, and vice versa. The golden rule is never be afraid to contact someone, even if superficially there would appear to be no direct link; they may have a piece of advice or information which could prove indispensable. Undertaking the necessary research to obtain as much relevant knowledge as possible before embarking on any project is very worthwhile, and in the longer term it will prove economic and efficient.

Education and training

Comprehensive education and training for event managers is still difficult to get, but the picture is beginning to look brighter. Having gone through years of virtually no opportunities to gain this sort of education and training, there are now a variety of courses at different levels to help event managers. And a variety of agencies (including ILAM) offer one-, two- or three-day in-service or in-house training sessions and conferences for practitioners.

Further education colleges offer GNVQ and Higher National opportunities in leisure and tourism, and related areas. The higher education sector runs a large number of courses in sports, leisure, the arts and other areas, courses which include units on event management. And there are closely related courses in project management. The development of vocational qualifications in event organisation and management has been championed by a variety of agencies, and although not available now, they certainly will be soon. On top of this, there are specific courses in first aid, health and safety, crowd control, etc.

There are now real opportunities for students and practitioners of event management to benefit from one-day courses and postgraduate study. This indicates the growth of the business and the response of educationalists. Today's opportunities to learn are not just about the mistakes of others.

Practical advice

Here are some key pieces of advice, anecdotes and golden rules picked up during research and over years of working in events. They offer real, practical assistance and will act as an added aide-mémoire for event organisers. I've left out the unprintable ones.

- Quality is the aim, not quantity.
- You've got to keep control of the expenditure.
- Always learn from the mistakes of others, not your own.
- Don't reinvent the wheel, there's usually someone whose been there before.
- Every event is somebody's first.

- We are all here for the audience/spectators/players.
- People are the key to successful events.
- If you can't do it well, don't do it at all.
- With hard work, thought, people management and planning comes success.
- Good publicity is vital; no one will come if they don't hear about it.
- Don't reach for the sky if the ceiling is good enough.
- Volunteers are good servants but terrible masters.
- Event skills are transferable, e.g. sports to heritage or vice versa.
- Attention to detail shows caring – and it works, even if it isn't noticed all the time.
- Remember humans are fallible. Write everything down; the key organiser could get knocked down by a bus.
- A good announcer's worth their weight in gold.
- Double-check everything!
- It *won't* be alright on the night.
- Don't make presentations or event closing ceremonies too long. They leave a bad impression even of a good event.
- Every event needs a troubleshooter or firefighter, someone who bullies to get things done.
- It doesn't matter how good a team you've got; if you have a weak coordinator, the event will not succeed.
- The problem with trying to estimate your budget is that you always get the unexpected expenditure.
- A pleasant decor – well thought out or appropriate and balanced – is essential to appealing events.
- An informative programme is vital to keep the audience interested and informed.
- Attention to detail cannot be overemphasised.
- Organising an event is rather like doing a gigantic jigsaw puzzle – juggling the pieces around, knowing they'll all fit in the end. Just make sure that you have all the pieces ready to fit in, when they are required.
- No matter how careful your planning, there is always something unexpected that happens.
- Keep staff fully in the picture; meet regularly for brief updates.
- Put all agreements in writing.
- Each event must have its 'chief executive' – a politician, a diplomat, a ruthless manager, a financial wizard, a 'man' of many parts.
- Involve your sponsor.
- I'd rather have twenty-five people who are prepared to sacrifice life to make an event happen, than one thousand who are there for the experience.
- The majority of major events are gliding smoothly across the surface, with a hell of a lot of paddling going on underneath.
- Be pessimistic in budgeting; not optimistic, not realistic, but pessimistic.

- A sense of humour is essential; it won't happen if it's too serious, the organisers will crack up. Humour helps keep the event in perspective.
- You've got to be able to think on your feet.
- Details, details, details!

Relevant books

It is difficult to obtain specifically relevant publications, but the following have been of use to me and may be helpful to other event organisers. Many texts on business management and organisation are also relevant to even management, especially if they cover project management.

- Allan J. (1989) *How to Develop Your Personal Management Skills,* Kogan Page, London
- American Sport Education Program (1996) *Event Management for Sport Directors,* Human Kinetics Publishers, Champaign IL
- Armstrong M. (1990) *Management Processes and Functions,* Short Run Press, Exeter
- Badmin P., Coombs M. and Rayner G. (1988) *Leisure Operational Management 1: Facilities,* Longman/ILAM, Harlow, England
- Batra P. (1995) *Management Thoughts,* Golden Books Centre, Kuala Lumpur
- Batterham G. (ed) (1992) *A Practical Approach to the Administration of Leisure and Recreation Services,* 4th edn, Croner Publications, Kingston upon Thames
- Briner W., Geddes M. and Hastings C. (1990) *Project Leadership,* Gower, Aldershot
- Brown M. (1992) *Successful Project Management in a Week,* Hodder & Stoughton, London
- Brown P. and Hackett F. (1990) *Managing Meetings,* Collins, London
- Buttrick R. (1997) *The Project Workout,* Pitman, London
- Byl J. (1990) *Organizing Successful Tournaments,* Leisure Press, Champaign IL
- Central Council of Physical Recreation (1990) *Let's Make an Event of It – Conferences, Seminars, Competitions, Training Schools and Fetes,* CCPR, London
- Cole G.A. (1993) *Management: Theory and Practice,* 4th edn, Guernsey Press, London
- Coltman M.M. (1989) *Tourism Marketing,* Van Nostrand Reinhold, New York
- Crainer S. (ed) (1995) *The Financial Times Handbook of Management – The State of the Art,* Pitman, London
- Daily Telegraph (1986) *How to Set Up and Run Conferences and Meetings,* Telegraph Publications, London
- Davis K.A. (1994) *Sport Management: Successful Private Sector Business Strategies,* Brown & Benchmark, Wisconsin MI
- Department of Trade and Industry (1998) *Fireworks – A Guide for Organisers of Public Displays,* DTI, London
- Druce R. and Carter S. (1998) *The Marketing Handbook – A Guide for Voluntary and Non-Profit Making Organisations,* National Extension College, Cambridge
- English Tourist Board, *The Give and Take of Sponsorship,* Eisenberg R. and Kelly K. (1986) *Organise Yourself,* Piatkus, London ETB, London
- English Tourist Board, *How to Organise an Event,* ETB, London

● English Tourist Board, *Putting on the Style*, ETB, London

● Festival Welfare Services (1990) *Co-ordinating Welfare Services at Festivals*, Festival Welfare Services, London

● Fleming I. (1994) *Training Needs Analysis for the Leisure Industry*, Longman, Harlow, England

● Goldblatt J.J. (1990) *Special Events: The Arts and Science of Celebration*, Van Nostrand Reinhold, New York

● Goldblatt J.J. (1997) *Special Events: Best Practices in Modern Event Management*, 2nd edn, Van Nostrand Reinhold, New York

● Hall C.M. (1992) *Hallmark Tourist Events – Impacts, Management and Planning*, Belhaven Press, London

● Hall L. (1977) *Meetings – Their Law and Practice*, MacDonald and Evans, Plymouth

● Haynes M.E. (1989) *Project Management – From Idea to Implementation*, Kogan Page, London

● Haywood L. (ed) (1994) *Community Leisure and Recreation*, Butterworth-Heinemann, Oxford

● Head V. (1984) *Successful Sponsorship*, Fitzwilliam Publishing, London

● Health and Safety Commission (1991) *A Guide to Health, Safety and Welfare at Pop Concerts and Other Similar Events*, HMSO, London

● Health and Safety Executive (1988) *Essentials of Health & Safety at Work*, HMSO, London

● Health and Safety Executive (1995) *Giving Your Own Firework Display*, HMSO, London

● Health and Safety Executive (1996) *Managing Crowds Safely*, HMSO, London

● Henry I.P. (ed) (1990) *Management & Planning in the Leisure Industries*, Macmillan, Basingstoke

● Hill T. (1993) *The Essence of Operations Management*, Prentice Hall, Hemel Hempstead, England

● Home Office and Scottish Office (1990) *Guide to Safety at Sports Grounds*, HMSO, London

● Hughes C. (1987) *Production & Operations Management*, Pan Books, London

● Inskeep E. (1991) *Tourism Planning*, Van Nostrand Reinhold, New York

● Jeferson A. and Lickorish L. (1991) *Marketing Tourism*, 2nd edn, Harlow, England

● Johns T. (1994) *Perfect Customer Care – All you Need to Get it Right First Time*, Arrow Business Books, London

● Jubenville A., Twight B.W. and Becker R.H. (1989) *Outdoor Recreation Management*, E & FN Spon, London

● Lance S. and Lance J. (produced annually) *The Showman's Directory*, Brook House, Surrey

● Lawrie A. (1996) *The Complete Guide to Creating & Managing New Projects for Charities & Voluntary Organisations*, Directory of Social Change, London

● Leslie D. (ed) (1995) *Tourism and Leisure – Perspectives on Provision*, LSA Publications, Eastbourne

● Lewis D. (1995) *10 Minute Time and Stress Management – How to Gain an 'Extra' 10 Hours a Week!* Piatkus, London

● Lock D. (1992) *Project Managment*, 5th edn, Gower, Aldershot

● Melnike C.J. and Wilkinson D.G. (1992) *Community Services Marketing*, Wilkinson Information Group Inc and Marketing Minds International, Ontario

● Passingham S. (1993) *Organising Local Events*, Directory of Social Change, London

● Rees N. (ed) (1993) *Dictionary of Modern Quotations*, Chambers, Edinburgh

● Rowntree D. (1996) *The Manager's Book of Checklists – Instant Management Solutions When You Need Them*, Pitman, London

● Rutherford D. (1990) *Introduction to the Conventions, Expositions and Meetings Industry*, Van Nostrand Reinhold, New York

● Sayers P. (1991) *Managing Sport and Leisure Facilities – A Guide to Competitive Tendering*, E & FN Spon, London

● Scott M. (1985) *The Law of Public Leisure Services*, Sweet and Maxwell, London

● Scott M. (1988) *Law and Leisure Services Management*, Longman, London

● Scottish Sports Council (1980) *Major Events – An Organisation Manual*, SSC, Edinburgh

● Seekings D. (1989) *How to Organise Effective Conferences and Meetings*, Kogan Page, London

● Sessoms H.D. and Stevenson J.L. (1981) *Leadership and Group Dynamics in Recreation Services*, Allyn & Bacon, Boston

● Sports Council (1978) *Public Disorder and Sporting Events*, Sports Council, London

● Stier W.F. Jr (1994) *Fundraising for Sport and Recreation – Step-by-Step Plans for 70 Successful Events*, Human Kinetics Publishers, Champaign IL

● Stone M. and Young L. (1992) *Competitive Customer Care – A Guide to Keeping Customers*, Croner Publications, Kingston upon Thames

● Tancred B. and Tancred G. (1992) *Leisure Management*, Hodder & Stoughton, London

● Taylor L. and Outhart T. (1996) *Developing Customer Service in Leisure and Tourism for Advanced GNVQ*, HarperCollins, London

● Thomas E. and Woods M. (1992) *The Manager's Casebook*, Duncan Petersen Publishing, London

● Torkildsen G. (1991) *Leisure and Recreation Management*, 2nd edn, E & FN Spon, London

● Tschohl J. (1996) *Achieving Excellence Through Customer Service*, 2nd edn, Advantage Quest Publications, Petaling Jaya, Malaysia

● Watt D.C. (1992) *Leisure & Tourism Events Management & Organisation Manual*, Longman, Harlow, England

● White A. (1995) *Managing for Performance – How to Get the Best out of Yourself and Your Team*, Piatkus, London

● Wilkinson D. (1988) *The Event Management & Marketing Institute 1*, IBD, Ontario

● Wright J. (1989) *Recreation & Leisure – City and Guilds Course 481 (Parts 1 and 2)*, Croner Publications, Kingston upon Thames

Journals, reports and proceedings

● *Aspects of Britain – Sport and Leisure* (1994) HMSO, London

● *The CCL Guide*, Conference Care Limited, London

● *Code of Practice for Outdoor Events – Other Than Pop Concerts and Raves* (January 1993) National Outdoor Events Association, Wallington, Surrey

● *Customer Service Park for the Leisure Industry* (1992) Longman, Harlow, England

● *The Directory of Grant Making Trusts*, Aid Foundation, Kent

● *The Directory of Social Change*, HarperCollins, London

- *Events Services Manual*, Victoria Conference Centre, Victoria BC
- *The Exhibition Data Book*, Reed Information Services, Sutton, Surrey
- *Hobsons Sponsorship Year Book*, Hobson's Publishing, London
- *Journal of Sport Management*, vol. 10, no. 3 (July 1996) Human Kinetics Publishers, Leeds
- *Journal of Sport Management*, vol. 11, no. 3 (July 1997) Human Kinetics Publishers, Leeds
  Leisure Services Year Book, Longman, Harlow, England
- *Marketing Leisure Services*, Leisure Futures, London
- *Outdoor Events Guide* (annual) Outdoor Events Publications, Wallington, Surrey
- *Shades of Green – Working Towards Green Tourism in the Countryside* (1990 conference proceedings) Fielder Green Associates, London
- *Victoria Conference Centre Conference Planning Checklist*, Victoria Conference Centre, Victoria BC
- *Voluntary but not Amateur – A Guide to the Law for Voluntary Organisations and Community Groups*, 4th edn (Oct 1994) London Voluntary Service Council, London
- Various publications of the Arts Councils and Sports Councils of England, Scotland, Wales and Northern Ireland

Other periodicals

Besides the titles on this list, there are literally hundreds of consumer periodicals which may be relevant to a specific event or some aspect of it. Perhaps a major caravan event is planned or specialist computer information is required. Each of these two fields is covered by a wide range of publications, and similar topics have their own selections.

Arts Management
Rhinegold Publishing
241 Shaftsbury Avenue
London WC2H 9AHJ
Tel: 0171 836 2534

Art Monthly
36 Great Russell Street
London WC1B 3PP
Tel: 0171 580 4168

Amateur Stage
83 George Street
London W1H 5PL
Tel: 0171 486 1732

Catering & Hotel Keeper
Reed Business Publishing Group
Quadrant House
The Quadrant
Sutton
Surrey SM2 5AS
Tel: 0181 661 8680

Conference & Marketplace
Angel Publishing Ltd
Kingsland House
361 City Road
London EC1V 1LR
Tel: 0171 417 7400

Conference & Seminar Selector Pack
Target Response
1 Riverside, Church Street
Edenbridge
Kent TN8 5BH
Tel: 01732 866122

Marketing
Haymarket Marketing Publications
22 Lancaster Gate
London W2 3LY
Tel: 0181 943 5000

Haymarket Management Magazines
30 Lancaster Gate
London W2 3LP
Tel: 0181 943 5000

Exhibition Bulletin
266/272 Kirkdale
Sydenham
London SE26 4RZ
Tel: 0181 778 2288

Exhibitions and Conferences
York Publishing Company
70 Abingdon Place
London W8 6AP
Tel: 0171 937 6636

The Exhibitor
Conference & Travel Publications Ltd
Media House
The Square
Forest Row
East Sussex RH18 5ES
Tel: 01342 824044

Countryside Commission News
John Gower House
Crescent Place
Cheltenham
Gloucester GL50 3RA
Tel: 01242 521381

English Heritage Magazine
Anthony Harvey Associates
83 Clerkenwell Road
London EC1R 5AR
Tel: 0171 831 9363

Library Management
MCB University Press
62 Toller Lane
Bradford West Yorkshire BD8 9BY
Tel: 01274 499821

Leisure Manager
ILAM
Lower Basildon
Reading RG8 9NE
Tel: 01491 874800

Managing Leisure
E & FN Spon
2–6 Boundary Row
London SE1 8HN
Tel: 0171 865 0066

Museums Journal
34 Bloomsbury Way
London WC1A 2SF
Tel: 0171 404 4767

Museum Management & Curatorship
Butterworth Heinnmann Ltd
PO Box 63
Westbury House
Bury Street
Guildford
Surrey GU2 5BH
Tel: 01483 300966

Leisure Week
St Giles House
49/50 Poland Street
London W1V 4AX
Tel: 0171 287 5000

Leisure Management and Leisure
   Opportunities
Dicestar Limited
40 Bancroft
Hitchin SG5 1LA
Tel: 01462 431385

Leisure Futures
The Henley Centre for Forecasting
2–4 Tudor Street
Blackfriars
London EC4Y 0AA
Tel: 0171 353 9961

Leisure Recreation & Tourism Abstracts
CAB International
Wallingford
Oxfordshire OX10 8DE
Tel: 01491 321111

Leisure Sciences
Taylor & Francis Ltd
I Gunpowder Square
London EC4A 3DE
Tel: 0171 583 0581

Leisure Studies Journal
Chapman & Hall Ltd
2–6 Boundary Row
London SE1 8HN
Tel: 0171 865 0066

Recreation
ISRM
Giffard House
36–38 Sherrard Street
Melton Mowbray LE13 1XJ
Tel: 01664 65531

Sports Industry
B & M Publications
PO Box 13
Hereford House
Bridle Path
Croydon
Surrey CR9 4NL
Tel: 0181 680 4200

Sponsorship Insights
Hobsons Publishing
Europa House
St Martin's Street
London SW1P 2JT
Tel: 0171 336 6633

Sports & Leisure Equipment News
Peterson Publishing Co Ltd
Northbank
Berryhill Industrial Estate
Droitwich WR9 9BL
Tel: 01905 795564

The Stage & Television Today
Carson & Comerford Ltd
47 Bermondsey Street
London SE1 3XT
Tel: 0171 403 1818

Sponsorship News
Charterhouse Business Publications
PO Box 66
Wokingham RG11 4RQ
Tel: 01734 772770

The Tourism Society
26 Grosvenor Gardens
London SW1W 0DU
Tel: 0171 730 4380

Tourism Enterprise
English Tourist Board
Thames Tower
Black's Road
Hammersmith
London W6 9EL
Tel: 0181 846 9000

Tourism Management
Butterworth Heinnemann Ltd
PO Box 63
Westbury House
Bury Street
Guildford
Surrey GU2 5BH
Tel: 01483 300966

Travel & Tourism Analyst
The Economist Intelligence Unit Ltd
40 Duke Street
London W1A 1DW
Tel: 0171 493 6711

Useful contact addresses

Institute of Leisure and Amenity
    Management (ILAM)
ILAM House
Lower Basildon
Reading RG8 9NE
Tel: 01491 874800
Fax: 01491 874801
(A professional institute incorporating
    ILAM Services, who organise events for
    other agencies)

The National Outdoor Events Association
7 Hamilton Way
Wallington
Surrey SM6 9NJ
Tel: 0181 669 8121
Fax: 0181 647 1128

Arts Management Unit (Liverpool)
Institute of PA & M
Liverpool University
Roxby Building
Myrtle Street
Liverpool LG9 3BX
Tel: 0151 709 6022

SPRITO
24 Stephenson Way
London NW1 2HD
Tel: 0171 388 7755
Fax: 0171 388 9733

Association of British Chambers of
  Commerce
212A Shaftesbury Avenue
London WC2H 8EW
Tel: 0171 240 5831

International Special Events Society
7080 Hollywood Boulevard
Suite 410
Los Angeles
CA 90028
United States

National Council for Voluntary
  Organisations
Regents Wharf, All Saints Street
London N1 9RL
Tel: 0171 713 6161

The Marketing Resource Centre
11–13 Charterhouse Buildings
London EC1M 7AN

The Arts Council of Great Britain
105 Picadilly
London W1V 0AU
Tel: 0171 629 9495

The Association for Business Sponsorship
  of the Arts
Nutmeg House
60 Gainsford Street
Butler's Wharf
London SE1 2NY
Tel: 0171 378 8143

The Arts Council for Northern Ireland
181 Stran Millis Road
Belfast BT9 5DU
Tel: 01232 663591

Central Council of Physical Recreation
Frances House
Frances Street
London SW1P 1DE
Tel: 0171 828 3163

The Charity Commission
14 Ryder Place
London SW1Y 6AH
Tel: 0171 214 6000

The English Tourist Board/British Tourist
  Authority
Thames Tower
Black Road
London W6 9EL
Tel: 0181 846 9000

The Institute of Sports Sponsorship
Frances House
Frances Street
London SW1P 1DE
Tel: 0171 828 8771

Association of Business Sponsors of the
  Arts (Scotland)
Room 613
Scottish Post Office Board
Post Officer Headquarters Scotland
West Port House
102 West Port
Edinburgh, EH3 9HS
Tel: 0131 228 7346

The Scottish Arts Council
19 Charlotte Square
Edinburgh EH2 4DF
Tel: 0131 226 6051

The Scottish Sports Council
Caledonia House
South Gyle
Edinburgh EH12 9DQ
Tel: 0131 317 7200

The Sponsorship Association
32 Sekforde Street
Clerkenwell Green
London EC1R 0HH
Tel: 0171 251 2505

Sports Aid Foundation
16 Upper Woburn Place
London WC1H 0QN
Tel: 0171 387 9380

The UK Sports Council
Walkenden House
10 Melton Street
London NW1 2EB
Tel: 0171 380 8000
Fax: 0171 380 8025

The English Sports Council
16 Upper Woburn Place
London WC1H 0QN
Tel: 0171 388 1277

The Sports Council for Wales
Sophia Gardens
Cardiff CF1 9SW
Tel: 01222 39751

The Welsh Arts Council
9 Museum Place
Cardiff CF1 2NX
Tel: 01222 394711

The Scottish Film Council
74 Victoria Crescent Road
Dowanhill
Glasgow G12 9JN
Tel: 0141 334 4445

British Film Institute
Information and Documentation Dept.
21 Steven Street
London W1P 1PL
Tel: 0171 255 1444

National Coaching Foundation
4 College Close
Beckett Park
Leeds LS6 3QH
Tel: 0113 274 4802
Fax: 0113 275 5019

The Scottish Tourist Board
23 Ravelston Terrace
Edinburgh EH4 3EU
Tel: 0131 332 2433

The Northern Ireland Tourist Board
River House
48 High Street
Belfast BT1 2DS
Tel: 01232 231221

The Welsh Tourist Board
8/14 Bridge Street
Cardiff CF1 2EE
Tel: 01222 227281

The National Trust
36 Queen Anne's Gate
London SW1H 9AS
Tel: 0171 222 9251

The National Trust for Scotland
5 Charlotte Square
Edinburgh EH2 4DU
Tel: 0131 226 5922

English Heritage
The Historic Buildings and Monuments
   Commission
Fortress House
23 Saville Row
London W1X 2HE
Tel: 0171 734 6010

The Welsh Historic Monuments
9th Floor, Brunel House
2 Fitzalan Road
Cardiff CF2 1UY
Tel: 01222 465511

Historic Scotland
20 Brandon Street
Edinburgh EH3 5RA
Tel: 0131 244 3087

The Civic Trust
17 Carlton House Terrace
London SW1Y 5AW
Tel: 0171 930 0914

The Forestry Commission
231 Corstorphine Road
Edinburgh EH12 7AT
Tel: 0131 334 0303

The Nature Conservatory Council
North Minster House
Peterborough PE1 1UA
Tel: 01733 40345

The Countryside Commission
John Dower House
Crescent Place
Cheltenham GL50 3RA
Tel: 01244 2521381

The Countryside Commission Office
   for Wales
Ladywell House
Newton Powys SY16 1RD
Tel: 01686 626799

Scottish Natural Heritage
Battleby
Redgorton
Perth PH1 3EW
Tel: 01738 27921

Tourism Society
26 Grosvenor Gardens
London SW1W 0DU
Tel: 0171 730 4380

The Museums Association
34 Bloomsbury Way
London WC1A 2SF
Tel: 0171 404 4767

The Library Association
7 Ridgmount Street
London WC1 7AE
Tel: 0171 636 7543

Institute of Sport and Recreation
   Management (ISRM)
Gifford House
36/38 Sherrard Street
Melton Mowbray LE13 1XJ
Tel: 01664 65531

Recreation Managers Association
7 Burkinshaw Avenue
Rawmarsh
Rotheram S62 7QZ
Tel: 01709 522463

The Association of Playing Fields Officers
   and Landscape Managers
c/o ISRM
Gifford House
36/38 Sherrard Street
Melton Mowbray LE13 1XJ
Tel: 01664 65531

Exhibition Surveys
PO Box 7
Melton Mowbray
Leicestershire LE13 0BR
Tel: 01664 67666

The National Exhibitors Association
29 Market Square
Biggleswade SG18 8AQ
Tel: 01767 316255

The National Association of Exhibition
   Hall Owners
The National Exhibition Centre
Birmingham B40 1NT
Tel: 0121 780 4141

Exhibition Industry Federation
222 Market Towers
9 Elm Lane
London SW8 5NQ
Tel: 0171 498 3306

British Exhibition Venues Association
c/o Alexandria Palace
Wood Green
London N22 4AY
Tel: 0181 365 2121

The British Exhibition Contractors
   Association
Kingsmere House
Graham Road
London SW19 3SR
Tel: 0181 503 3888

The Association of Exhibition Organisers
207 Market Towers
9 Elm Lane
London SW8 5NQ

The Association of British Conference
   Organisers
Honorary Secretary Tony Waters
54 Church Street
Tilsbury
Salisbury SP3 6NH

The Association of Conference Executives
Riverside House
High Street
Huntingdon PE18 6SG
Tel: 01480 457595

The Association of British Chambers of
   Commerce
Sovereign House
212a Shaftsbury Avenue
London WC2H 8EW
Tel: 0171 240 5831

The Association of British Travel Agents
55–57 Newman Street
London W1P 4AH
Tel: 0171 637 2444

The Association of Exhibition Organisers
   Limited
9 Totteridge Avenue
High Wycombe HP13 6XG
Tel: 01494 30430

British Exhibition Contractors Association
Kingsmere House
Grayham Road
Wimbledon
London SW19 3SR
Tel: 0181 543 3888

Conference Managers Association
c/o Schwarzkopf Limited
Penn Road
Aylesbury HP21 8HL
Tel: 01296 88101

International Association for Professional
  Conference Organisers
40 Rue Washington
Brussels 1050
Belgium
Tel: 00 33 2 6401808

International Congress and Convention
  Association
International House
36 Dudley Road
Royal Tunbridge Wells TV1 1LB
Tel: 01892 42011

The National Association of Exhibition
  Organisers
2 Pelham Road
South Woodford
London E18 1PX
Tel: 0181 366 1291

The National Joint Council for the
  Exhibition Industry
Ucatt House
177 Abbeyville Road
London SW4 9RL
Tel: 0181 662 2442

Scottish Conference Association
Business Travel Department
Scottish Tourist Board
23 Ravelston Terrace
Edinburgh EH4 3EW
Tel: 0131 332 2433

Corporate Hospitality Association
PO Box 67
Kingswood
Hadworth
Surrey KT20 6LG
Tel: 017337 833963

The Mobile and Outside Caterers
  Association of Great Britian
17 Hamilton Way
Wallington SM6 9NG
Tel: 0181 669 8121

The Physical Education Association of
  Great Britain
Ling House
162 Kings Cross Road
London WC1X 9TH
Tel: 0171 278 9311

The National Playing Fields Association
25 Ovington Square
London SW3 1LQ
Tel: 0171 584 6445

The Scottish Games Association
Lime Tree Cottage
Pitcairn Green
Perth PH1 3LP
Tel: 01738 83754

British Olympic Association
1 Church Row
Wandsworth Plain
London SW18 1PH
Tel: 0181 874 8978

Charity Aid Foundation
48 Pembury Road
Tonbridge
Kent TN9 2JD
Tel: 01732 771333

British Music Society
53 High Street
Wells-next-the-Sea
Norfolk NR23 1EN
Tel: 01328 710552

British Federation of Music Festivals
Festivals House
198 Park Lance
Macclesfield SK11 6UD
Tel: 01625 28297

National Federation of Music Societies
Frances House
Frances Street
London SW1P 1DA
Tel: 0171 828 7320

The British Library
96 Euston Road
London NW1 2DB
Tel: 0171 412 7000

The National Library of Scotland
King George IV Bridge
Edinburgh EH1 1EW
Tel: 0131 636 1555

Museums and Galleries Commission
7 St James' Square
London SW1Y 4JU
Tel: 0171 839 9341

National Museums of Scotland
Chamber Street
Edinburgh EH1 1JF
Tel: 0131 225 7534

The National Gallery
Trafalgar Square
London WC2N 5ND
Tel: 0171 839 3321

The National Gallery of Scotland
Information Department
Belford Road
Edinburgh EH4 3DR
Tel: 0131 556 8921

The Photographers Gallery
Halina House
588 Great Newport Street
London WC2H 7HY
Tel: 0171 831 1772

Federation of British Artists
17 Carlton House Terrace
London SW1Y 5ED
Tel: 0171 930 6844

The National Museum of Photography,
    Film and Television
Princess View
Bradford BD5 0TR
Tel: 0127 727488

National Museum for Wales
Cathays Park
Cardiff CF1 3NP
Tel: 01222 397951

National Association of Decorative and
    Fine Arts Societies
38 Edbury Street
London SW1W 0LU
Tel: 0171 730 3042

The Royal Fine Art Commission
7 St James' Square
London SW1Y 4JU
Tel: 0171 839 6537

The Arts Business Initiative
City Hall
Barkers Pool
Sheffield S1 2HB
Tel: 01742 735926

The British Council
10 Spring Gardens
London SW1A 2BN
Tel: 0171 389 4938

The Design Council
28 Haymarket
London SW1Y 4SU
Tel: 0171 839 8000

The Design Council for Scotland
72 St Vincent's Street
Glasgow G2 5KN
Tel: 0141 221 6121

Crafts Council
44A Pentonville Road
London N1 9BY
Tel: 0171 278 7700

The Council for Regional Arts Associations
13a Clifton Road
Winchester SO22 5BP
Tel: 01962 51063

UNISON
1 Mabledon Place
London WC1H 9AJ
Tel: 0171 388 2366

Performing Rights Society Limited
29/33 Berner Street
London W1P 4AA
Tel: 0181 580 5544

British Association of Conference Towns
International House
43 Dudley Road
Royal Tunbridge Wells TN1 1LB

Recreational and Leisure Trade Association
Prudential House
10th Floor
Wellesley Road
Croydon CR0 9XY

British Hotels, Restaurants and Caterers
  Association
40 Duke Street
London W1M 6HR
Tel: 0171 499 6641

National Federation of Community
  Organisations
8/9 Upper Street
Islington
London N1 0PQ
Tel: 0171 226 0189

The Scottish Civic Trust
24 George Square
Glasgow G2 1EF
Tel: 0141 221 1466

The Civic Trust for Wales
Room 4
Llandaff Court
Fairwater Road
Llandaff
Cardiff CF5 2LN
Tel: 01222 522388

The Association of Metropolitan
  Authorities
35 Great Smith Street
Westminster
London SW1P 3BJ
Tel: 0171 222 8100

Convention on Scottish Local Authorities
  (COSLA)
Rosebury House
Haymarket Terrace
Edinburgh EH12 5XZ
Tel: 0131 374 9200

National Association for Local Councils
108 Great Russell Street
London WC1B 3LD
Tel: 0171 637 1865

The Association of District Councils
9 Buckingham Gate
London SW1A 6LE
Tel: 0171 828 7931

Hotel and Catering Training Board
International House
High Street
Ealing
London W5 5DB
Tel: 0181 579 2400

Local Government Training Board
Arndale House
Arndale Centre
Luton LU1 2TS
Tel: 01582 051166

Hotel, Catering and Institutional
  Management Association
191 Trinity Road
London SW17 7HN
Tel: 0181 672 4251

The Law Society
Law Society's Hall
113 Chancery Lane
London WC2A 1PL
Tel: 0171 242 1222

The Institute of Management
Africa House
64/78 Kingsway
London WC2 6BL
Tel: 0171 405 3456

Institute of Management Consultants
5th Floor
32/33 Hatton Garden
London EC1N 8DL
Tel: 0171 584 7285

The Market Research Society
175 Oxford Street
London W1R 1TA
Tel: 0171 439 2585

The Institute of Marketing
Moore Hall
Cookham
Maidenhead SL6 9QH
Tel: 01628 24922

British Institute of Professional
 Photography
2 Almwell End
Ware SG12 9HN
Tel: 01920 40111

Institute of Public Relations
Gatehouse
St John's Square
London EC1M 4DH
Tel: 0171 253 5151

Institute of Sales and Marketing
 Management
31 Upper George Street
Luton LU1 2RD
Tel: 01582 411130

Institute of Travel and Tourism
113 Victoria Street
St Albans AL1 3TJ
Tel: 01727 54395

British Theatre Association
Regents College
Inner Circle
Regents Park
London NW1 4NW
Tel: 0171 487 7700

Pre-School Learning Alliance
69 Kings Cross Road
London WC1X 9LL
Tel: 0171 833 0991

British Standards Institution
2 Park Street
London W1A 2BS
Tel: 0171 629 9000

Don't forget your telephone book, Yellow Pages and local directories (often handed out by the press and other media); they can prove invaluable. Your local library is a gold mine of valuable information.

Useful media addresses

BBC
Broadcasting House
Portland Place
London W1A 1AA

BBC TV
Television Centre
Wood Lane
London W12 1AA
Tel: 0181 743 8000

Association of Independent Producers Ltd
17 Great Pulteney Street
London W1R 3DG
Tel: 0171 434 0181

Association of Independent Producers
 (AIP)
Paramount House
162–170 Wardour Street
London W1V 4LA
Tel: 0171 434 0181

British Sky Broadcasting
6 Centairs Business Park
Grant Way
Isleworth
Middlesex TW9 5QD
Tel: 0171 782 3000

British Telecom International TV
Distribution Services (TVDS)
Room 723
Holborn Centre
London EC1N 2TE
Tel: 0171 492 2626/9

European Telecommunications Satellite
 Organisation (Eutelsat)
Tour Maine
Montparnasse
33 Avenue Du Maine
75755 Paris
Cedex 15
France
Tel: 00 331 45384747

Channel 4 TV Co Ltd
124 Horseferry Road
London SW1P 2TX
Tel: 0171 396 4444

Independent Broadcasting Authority (IBA)
70 Brompton Road
London SW3
Tel: 0171 584 7011

Independent Programme Producers
  Association (IPPA)
50–51 Berwick Street
London W1A 4RD
Tel: 0171 439 7034

Super Channel
New Media Sales Ltd
25 Soho Square
London W1V 5FJ
Tel: 0171 631 5050

The Cable Authority
Gillingham House
38–44 Gillingham Street
London SW1V 1HU
Tel: 0171 821 6161

Ceefax
Room 7059
BBC Television Centre
Wood Lane
London W12 7RJ
Tel: 0181 743 8000

Oracle Teletext
Craven House
25/32 Marshall Street
London W1V 1LL
Tel: 0171 434 3121

The European
200 Gray's Inn Road
London WC1X 8NG
Tel: 0171 418 7777

The Independent/Independent on Sunday
1 Canada Square
Canary Wharf
London E14 5DL
Tel: 0171 345 2000

Daily Telegraph/Sunday Telegraph
Peterborough Court
South Quay
181 Marsh Wall
London E14 9SR
Tel: 0171 538 5000

The Sun/News of the World
Virginia Street
London E1 9XR
Tel: 0171 782 4000

The Courier
7 Bank Street
Dundee DD1 9HU
Tel: 01382 23131

Daily Express/Sunday Express
Ludgate House
245 Blackfriars Road
London SE1 9UX
Tel: 0171 928 8000

Daily Mail/Mail on Sunday
Northcliffe House
2 Derry Street
London W8 5TT
Tel: 0171 938 6000

Daily Star
Ludgate House
245 Blackfriars Road
London SE1 9UX
Tel: 0171 928 8000

Daily Record/Sunday Mail
Anderston Quay
Glasgow G3 8DA
Tel: 0141 248 7000

The Guardian
164 Deansgate
Manchester M60 2RR
Tel: 0161 832 7200

The Times/Sunday Times
1 Pennington Street
London E1 0XN
Tel: 0171 782 5000

Daily Mirror/Sunday Mirror/The People
1 Canada Square
Canary Wharf
London E14 5AP
Tel: 0171 345 2000

The Observer
119 Farringdon Road
London EC1R 3ER
Tel: 0171 278 2332

The Herald
195 Albion Street
Glasgow G1 1QP
Tel: 0141 552 6255

Sunday Post
Courier Place
Dundee DD1 9QJ
Tel: 01382 23131

The Scotsman
20 North Bridge
Edinburgh EH1 1YT
Tel: 0131 225 2468

Index